D0065332

BLACK POWER:

the radical response
to white america

The Insight Series
Studies in Contemporary Issues
from Glencoe Press

Series Editors: Fred Krinsky and Joseph Boskin

BLACK POWER:
the radical response
to white america

Thomas Wagstaff

Assistant Professor
Department of History
Chico State College

GLENCOE PRESS
A Division of The Macmillan Company
Beverly Hills
Collier-Macmillan Ltd., London

First printing, 1969.

Library of Congress catalog card number: 70-76123

Glencoe Press.
A Division of The Macmillan Company.

Printed in the United States of America.

Collier-Macmillan Canada, Ltd., Toronto, Canada.

Preface

The historic aim of Negro protest movements in America has been the achievement of equal liberties, rights and status for all Americans, irrespective of race or color—a goal loosely summed up by the term "integration." To the extent that they have pursued integrationist programs, Black Americans have strongly affirmed their faith in the fundamental soundness of American principles and institutions. For to believe in the eventual accomplishment of racial integration, it is necessary to believe that racial discrimination, the consistent factor in American race relations for three-and-a-half centuries, is an historical anachronism, not an integral and definitive fact of life in America. The events of recent years have gravely shaken the foundations of that faith and given wide credence in the Black community to the conviction that racial prejudice, in its various manifestations, is and will continue to be the controlling reality of their lives. The result has been a powerful challenge to the integrationist philosophy and the emergence of the concept of Black Power— itself a broad term denoting a variety of not always compatible separatist and revolutionary goals.

The Swedish social scientist, Gunnar Myrdal, in his massive study of American race relations, *An American Dilemma*, provided the classic definition of the faith that underlies the integrationist program. Although his studies documented the prevalence of racism in every aspect of American life, Myrdal maintained that the American commitment to equality was the stronger force and would ultimately prevail.

> The bright side is that the conquering of color caste is America's own inherent desire. The nation early laid down as the moral basis for its existence the principles of equality and liberty. . . . The great reason for hope is that the country has a national experience of uniting racial and cultural diversities and a national theory, if not a consistent practice of freedom and equality for all. What America is constantly reaching for is

democracy at home and abroad. The main trend of its history is the gradual realization of the American creed.*

Hope in the potential fulfillment of that American creed heartened the Civil Rights Movement during its dramatic confrontation with the forces of institutionalized racism during the 1950's and 1960's. It inspired the stirring dream of the Movement's most striking figure, Martin Luther King, Jr., "that one day this nation will rise up and live out the true meaning of its creed: 'We hold these truths to be self-evident; that all men are created equal. . . .' " That faith also sustained King's belief that prejudice could be conquered by non-violent pressure on the conscience of the nation:

> When, for decades, you have been able to make a man compromise his manhood by threatening him with a cruel and unjust punishment, and when suddenly he turns upon you and says: "Punish me. I do not deserve it, I will accept it so that the world will know that I am right and you are wrong," you hardly know what to do. You feel defeated and secretly ashamed. You know that this man is as good a man as you are.†

Armed only with the American creed, protected only by faith in the ultimate good conscience of White America, Black men, women, and children carried the fight for equality into the courts and streets of the nation and won sweeping symbolic victories. In the decade that began with the Supreme Court's 1954 decision outlawing school segregation and ended with the enactment of the far-reaching Civil Rights Act of 1964, virtually all the legal bulwarks of racial discrimination were swept aside.

Yet despite those legal and moral victories, won at terrible costs in effort and blood, the gap between Black and White America remained tragically wide and seemed to be widening. Continuing and rapidly worsening de facto residential and educational segregation in every major northern urban center made a mockery of the infinitesimal progress towards integration in the southern states. The relative employment levels and earning power of Black workers deteriorated rather than improved. Between 1964 and 1968 the simmering rage in the rotting ghetto slums of numerous northern cities periodically exploded in severe race riots. In 1968 the President's National Advisory Commission appointed to investigate those civil disorders forthrightly attributed them to "the racial attitudes and behavior of White Americans toward Black Americans," and warned that if racism and its effects were not erased "large-scale and continuing violence could result, followed by White retaliation, and, ultimately the separation of the two communities in a garrison state."**

---

* Gunnar Myrdal, *An American Dilemma* (New York: Harper & Row; 1944), p. 1021.

† Martin Luther King, "I Have A Dream," Address to The March on Washington for Jobs and Freedom, Washington, D.C., August 28, 1963; King, *Why We Can't Wait* (New York: Harper & Row, 1964), p. 19.

** *New York Times* (March 1, 1968).

In the mingled optimism and frustration of the 1960's, Black Nationalism, the radical alternative to integration, a constant, if muted theme in the history of Negro protest thought in America, made a powerful appeal to the Black community.

The Black protest movement took a drastic turn in the summer of 1966. James Meredith, a Negro activist who had broken the color bar at the University of Mississippi four years earlier, was shot and wounded while attempting a "walk against fear" through the heart of the bitterly segregationist Mississippi River Delta region. Shortly thereafter several civil-rights groups organized a protest march towards Jackson, Mississippi, Meredith's projected goal. During the course of that march, a spellbinding young orator named Stokely Carmichael, newly elected head of the Student Non-Violent Coordinating Committee, riveted the attention of the nation on his demand for Black Power. Thrusting aside the counsels and the programs of established spokesmen like King and Roy Wilkins of the NAACP, Carmichael galvanized his rural audiences with strident appeals to race pride and abrasive demands for separate Black economic and political action. Before the march ended, Carmichael had sparked a national controversy about the opposing concepts of Black Nationalism and integration. The Civil Rights Movement in America had entered a dramatic new phase.

On one side of the ensuing debate, integrationist-minded Negro leaders and their White liberal sympathizers continued, as novelist James Baldwin put it, to "point to a new day which is coming in America." But, Baldwin said,

> this day has been coming for nearly one hundred years. Viewed solely in the light of this country's moral professions, this lapse is inexcusable. Even more important, however, is that fact that there is desperately little in the record to indicate that white America ever seriously desired—or desires—to see this day arrive.*

The Black Nationalist assertion that it was the material substance of racism and not the rhetoric of equality that defined the reality of American life had, Baldwin stated, "all the evidence on its side." Other observers shared that somber view. Charles Silberman, reviewing the racial scene in the 1960's, wrote that it was no longer possible to believe in the "American Dilemma" as Myrdal had defined it.

> The tragedy of race relations in the United States is that there is no American Dilemma. White Americans are not torn and tortured by the conflict between their devotion to the American creed and their actual behavior. They are upset by the current state of race relations, to be sure. But what troubles them is not that justice is being denied but that their peace is being shattered and their business interrupted.†

---

* James Baldwin, *Nobody Knows My Name* (New York: Dial Press, 1961), p. 70.

† Charles Silberman, *Crisis in Black and White* (New York: Vintage Books, 1964), pp. 9–10.

In its forthright acceptance of that situation, the Black Power Movement found its most fundamental strength. It is, Black Nationalists argue persuasively, foolhardy and degrading for Black people to continue to place their trust in the eventual fulfillment of America's egalitarian ideals. "Being born here in America doesn't make you an American," said Malcolm X, the most effective of the Black Nationalist spokesmen. "Why if birth made you an American, you wouldn't need any legislation, you wouldn't need any amendments to the Constitution."

Stokely Carmichael stated that Black people would no longer uphold the traditions that had been dishonored by White Americans. "We can't be expected any longer to march and get our heads broken to say to you that you are nice guys," he declared. "You are not nice guys. We have found you out. You are rotten through and through ————. That's what we're saying."*

The proponents of Black Power argue that the Black community should reject integration as a goal and nonviolence as a required tactic. They maintain that Black people must achieve control of their own lives and the institutions that affect them. The advocates of the many variants of Black Power or Black Nationalism include mystical religious seers, pragmatic students of traditional American interest-bloc politics, and radical exponents of revolutionary socialist theories. Their combined influence in the American Negro community, particularly with the younger generation, has expanded enormously in recent years and is certain to have drastic effects on the course of race relations and thus on the general stability and direction of American society in the immediate future.

The documents contained in this book are intended to provide some insight into the intellectual background of Black Power. The selections in Chapter One are designed to illustrate the Negroes' historical attempts to identify themselves with the mainstream of American life and to show some of the psychological and cultural effects of their inability to do so. The documents in Chapter Two reflect the radical tradition in American Negro protest thought as it developed in the nineteenth century. Chapter Three explores nationalist and revolutionary influences in the early twentieth century. Chapter Four presents the writings of the modern adherents of Black Power and concludes with some scholarly analyses of its meaning and direction.

T.W.

Chico, California
September, 1968

---

* Quoted in Fred Powledge, *Black Power, White Resistance* (Cleveland: World Publishing Co., 1967), p. 241.

(NOTE.—Throughout this book, the author–editor's footnotes are marked by symbols—*, †—and the original quoted notes by numerals.)

Contents

Chapter One

The Negroes' Quest for an American Identity

Throughout the history of the United States, American Negroes have generally identified themselves with the values and institutions of the nation and have ardently sought to win recognition for themselves as Americans. Unlike the other ethnic groups that founded this "nation of immigrants," Black people did not come here seeking the freedom or opportunity to fulfill self-defined economic, political, religious, or social ambitions. They came involuntarily, as captive slaves, under conditions that stripped them of their previous cultural heritage and prevented them from developing either a strong sense of ethnic identity or a feeling of group solidarity. More completely than any other national or ethnic group they were divested of their original ideas and habits and forced to adapt to distinctly American attitudes and behavior patterns.* Thus they have usually responded to the constant economic exploitation and social prejudice to which they have been subjected in America by appealing to America's long-deferred commitments to the principles of "liberty and justice for all,"—that is, by asking for redress from, and in terms of, the system that has created and perpetuated their grievances.

---

* Stanley Elkins, *Slavery: A Problem in American Institutional Life* (Chicago: Grosset & Dunlap, 1959).

One of the most poignant effects of America's refusal to grant those pleas for acceptance has been a pervading attitude of individual and group self-contempt in the Negro community. Other minority groups, preserving the sense of a common and respected heritage, have been able to draw closer together in the face of adversity and mount concerted countermeasures. The Negroes' frustration and anger at their continued exploitation and rejection has generally been directed not at their oppressors, but turned inward upon themselves. E. Franklin Frazier, in his study of the attitudes of the Black middle class, noted this phenomenon and its manifestations.

> While pretending to be proud of being a Negro, they ridicule Negroid physical characteristics and seek to modify or efface them as much as possible. Within their own group they constantly proclaim that "niggers" make them sick. . . . They talk condescendingly of Africans and of African culture. . . . They are insulted if they are identified with Africans. They refuse to join organizations that are interested in Africa. . . . If a Black woman has European features they will remark condescendingly, "Although she is Black, you must admit that she is good-looking." . . . They studiously avoid association with other Negroes, especially if they themselves have received the slightest recognition by Whites. Even when they can not pass for White they fear that they will lose this recognition if they are identified as Negroes.*

Novelist James Baldwin states that "one of the prices an American Negro pays—or can pay—for what is called his 'acceptance' is a profound, almost ineradicable self-hatred. This corrupts every aspect of his living, he is never at peace again, he is out of touch with himself forever."†

In recent years an increasingly large number of Negroes has begun to consciously confront this problem. The appeal of the Black Power Movement lies principally in its extremely effective attack on the cultural and psychological sources of the identity crisis of American Negroes. Its advocates call on Black people to repudiate their loyalty to a society which rejects them, to rediscover and take pride in their African past, to accept their color as a badge of honor rather than of shame and to use it as the basis for united social, economic, and political action.

---

* E. Franklin Frazier, *Black Bourgeoisie* (New York: The Macmillan Company, 1957), pp. 226–227.

† Baldwin, *Nobody Knows My Name*, p. 170.

Under the Abuse and Censure of the World (1792)*

Benjamin Banneker

Benjamin Banneker (1731–1806), a free Negro from Maryland, was a self-educated mathematical genius. He made important contributions to the study of astronomy, published a series of widely respected scientific almanacs and served on the commission that surveyed the site of Washington, D.C. He sent the following letter to his fellow scientist, Thomas Jefferson, then secretary of state, to refute Jefferson's influential observations on the mental inferiority of the Negro.

I am fully sensible of that freedom which I take with you in the present occasion; a liberty which seemed to me scarcely allowable when I reflected on that distinguished and dignified station in which you stand, and the almost general prejudice and prepossession which is so prevalent in the world against those of my complexion.

I suppose it is a truth, too well attested to you to need a proof here, that we are a race of beings who have long labored under the abuse and censure of the world; that we have long been looked upon with an eye of contempt; and that we have long been considered rather as brutish than human, and scarcely capable of mental endowments.

Sir, I hope I may safely admit, in consequence of that report which hath reached me, that you are a man less inflexible in sentiments of this nature than many others; that you are measurably friendly, and well disposed towards us; and that you are willing and ready to lend your aid and assistance to our relief from those many distresses and numerous calamities to which we are reduced.

Now, Sir, if this is founded in truth, I apprehend you will embrace every opportunity to eradicate that train of absurd and false ideas and opinions which so generally prevails with respect to us; and that your sentiments are concurrent with mine, which are that one universal Father hath given being to us all; and that He hath

* Benjamin Banneker to Thomas Jefferson, Philadelphia, 1792, in Herbert Aptheker, *A Documentary History of the Negro People in the United States: From Colonial Times Through the Civil War* (New York: The Citadel Press, 1951), pp. 23–26.

not only made us all of one flesh, but that He hath also, without partiality, afforded us all the same sensations and endowed us all with the same faculties; and that however variable we may be in society or religion, however diversified in situation or color, we are all in the same family and stand in the same relation to Him.

Sir, if these are sentiments of which you are fully persuaded, I hope you cannot but acknowledge that it is the indispensable duty of those who maintain for themselves the rights of human nature, and who possess the obligations of Christianity, to extend their power and influence to the relief of every part of the human race, from whatever burden or oppression they may unjustly labor under; and this, I apprehend, a full conviction of the truth and obligation of these principles should lead all to.

Sir, I have long been convinced that if your love for yourselves, and for those inestimable laws which preserved to you the rights of human nature, was founded on sincerity, you could not but be solicitous that every individual, of whatever rank or distinction, might with you equally enjoy the blessings thereof; neither could you rest satisfied short of the most active effusion of your exertions in order to [effect] the promotion from any state of degradation to which the unjustifiable cruelty and barbarism of men may have reduced them.

Sir, I freely and cheerfully acknowledge that I am of the African race, and in that color which is natural to them of the deepest dye; and it is under a sense of the most profound gratitude to the Supreme Ruler of the universe that I now confess to you that I am not under that state of tyrannical thralldom and inhuman captivity to which too many of my brethren are doomed, but that I have abundantly tasted of the fruition of those blessings which proceed from that free and unequalled liberty with which you are favored; and which, I hope, you will willingly allow you have mercifully received from the immediate hand of that Being from whom proceedeth every good and perfect gift.

Sir, suffer me to recall to your mind, that time in which the arms and tyranny of the British Crown were exerted, with every powerful effort, in order to reduce you to a state of servitude; look back, I entreat you, on the variety of dangers to which you were exposed; reflect on that time in which every human aid appeared unavailable and in which even hope and fortitude wore the aspect of inability to the conflict, and you cannot but be led to a serious and grateful sense of your miraculous and providential preservation; you cannot but acknowledge that the present freedom and tranquility which you enjoy you have mercifully received, and that it is the peculiar blessing of Heaven.

This, Sir, was a time when you clearly saw into the injustice of a state of slavery, and in which you had just apprehensions of the horror of its condition. It was now that your abhorrence thereof was so excited that you publicly held forth this true and invaluable doctrine which is worthy to be recorded and remembered in all succeeding ages: "We hold these truths to be self-evident, that all men are created equal; that they are endowed by their Creator with certain unalienable rights, and that among these are, life, liberty, and the pursuit of happiness."

Here was a time in which your tender feelings for yourselves had engaged you thus to declare you were then impressed with proper ideas of the great violation of liberty and the free possession of those blessings to which you were entitled by nature; but, Sir, how pitiable is it to reflect that although you were so fully convinced of the benevolence of the Father of Mankind, and of His equal and impartial distribution of these rights and privileges which He hath conferred upon them, that you should at the same time counteract His mercies in detaining by fraud and violence so numerous a part of my brethren under groaning captivity and cruel oppression, that you should at the same time be found guilty of that most criminal act which you professedly detested in others with respect to yourselves.

I suppose that your knowledge of the situation of my brethren is too extensive to need a recital here; neither shall I presume to prescribe methods by which they may be relieved, otherwise than by recommending to you and all others to wean yourselves from those narrow prejudices which you have imbibed with respect to them, and as Job proposed to his friends, "Put your soul in their souls' stead"; thus shall your hearts be enlarged with kindness and benevolence towards them; and thus shall you need neither the direction of myself or others in what manner to proceed herein.

And now, Sir, although my sympathy and affection for my brethren hath caused my enlargement thus far, I ardently hope that your candor and generosity will plead with you in my behalf when I make known to you that it was not originally my design;

but having taken up my pen in order to direct to you, as a present, a copy of my Almanac which I have calculated for the succeeding year, I was unexpectedly and unavoidably led thereto.

This calculation is the product of my arduous study, in this most advanced stage of life; for having long had unbounded desires to become acquainted with the secrets of nature, I have had to gratify my curiosity herein through my own assiduous application to astronomical study, in which I need not recount to you the many difficulties and disadvantages which I have had to encounter.

Why Am I a Slave?*

Frederick Douglass

Frederick Douglass (1817–1895) was the most widely known and respected Negro spokesman of the nineteenth century. Born in slavery, he escaped in 1838 and became one of the most effective leaders of the Abolitionist Movement. A brilliant orator and author, his autobiographical accounts of slavery were of enormous value to the antislavery cause. After the Civil War and Emancipation, he continued to be an influential proponent of the rights and dignity of Black people in America.

The incidents related in the foregoing chapter led me thus early to inquire into the origin and nature of slavery. Why am I a slave? Why are some people slaves and others masters? These were perplexing questions and very troublesome to my childhood. I was very early told by someone that "God up in the sky" had made all things, and had made Black people to be slaves and White people to be masters. I was told too that God was good, and that He knew what was best for everybody. This was, however, less satisfactory than the first statement. It came point-blank against all my notions of goodness. . . . Besides, I could not tell how anybody could know that God made Black people to be slaves. Then I found, too, that there were puzzling exceptions to this theory of slavery, in the fact that

---

* Frederick Douglass, *The Life and Times of Frederick Douglass* (Boston: De Wolfe, Fiske and Company, 1892), pp. 56–59.

all Black people were not slaves, and all White people were not masters.

An incident occurred about this time that made a deep impression on my mind. My Aunt Jennie and one of the men slaves of Captain Anthony ran away. A great noise was made about it. Old master was furious. He said he would follow them and catch them and bring them back, but he never did, and somebody told me that Uncle Noah and Aunt Jennie had gone to the free states and were free. Besides this occurrence, which brought much light to my mind on the subject, there were several slaves on Mr. Lloyd's place who remembered being brought from Africa. There were others who told me that their fathers and mothers were stolen from Africa.

This to me was important knowledge, but not such as to make me feel very easy in my slave condition. The success of Aunt Jennie and Uncle Noah in getting away from slavery was, I think, the first fact that made me seriously think of escape for myself. I could not have been more than seven or eight years old at the time of this occurrence, but young as I was I was already, in spirit and purpose, a fugitive from slavery.

Up to the time of the brutal treatment of my Aunt Esther, already narrated, and the shocking plight in which I had seen my cousin from Tuckahoe, my attention had not been especially directed to the grosser and more revolting features of slavery. I had, of course, heard of whippings and savage mutilations of slaves by brutal overseers, but happily for me I had always been out of the way of such occurrences. My playtime was spent outside of the corn and tobacco fields, where the overseers and slaves were brought together and in conflict. But after the case of my Aunt Esther I saw others of the same disgusting and shocking nature. The one of these which agitated and distressed me most was the whipping of a woman, not belonging to my old master, but to Colonel Lloyd. The charge against her was very common and very indefinite, namely, "impudence." This crime could be committed by a slave in a hundred different ways, and depended much upon the temper and caprice of the overseer as to whether it was committed at all. He could create the offense whenever it pleased him. A look, a word, a gesture, accidental or intentional, never failed to be taken as impudence when he was in the right mood for such an offense. In this case there were all the necessary conditions for the commission of the crime charged. The offender was nearly white, to begin with; she was the wife of a favorite hand on board of Mr. Lloyd's sloop, and was besides, the mother of five sprightly children. Vigorous and spirited woman that she was, a wife and a mother, with a predominating share of the blood of the master running in her veins, Nellie (for that was her name) had all the qualities essential to impudence to a slave overseer. My attention was called to the scene of the castigation by the loud screams and curses that proceeded from the direction of it. When I came near the parties engaged in the struggle the overseer had hold of Nellie, endeavoring with his whole strength to drag her to a tree against her resistance. Both his and her faces were bleeding, for the woman was doing her best. Three of her children were present, and though quite small (from seven to ten years old, I should think), they gallantly took the side of their mother against the overseer, and pelted him well with stones and epithets. Amid the screams of the children, *"Let my mammy go! Let my mammy go!"* the hoarse voice of the maddened overseer was heard in terrible oaths that he would teach her how to give a White man "impudence." The blood on his face and on hers attested her skill in the use of her nails, and his dogged determination to conquer. His purpose was to tie her up to a tree and give her, in slaveholding parlance, a "genteel flogging," and he evidently had not expected the stern and protracted resistance he was meeting or the strength and skill needed to its execution. There were times when she seemed likely to get the better of the brute, but he finally overpowered her and succeeded in getting her arms firmly tied to the tree towards which he had been dragging her. The victim was now at the mercy of his merciless lash. What followed I need not here describe. The cries of the now helpless woman, while undergoing the terrible infliction, were mingled with the hoarse curses of the overseer and the wild cries of her distracted children. When the poor woman was untied her back was covered with blood. She was whipped, terribly whipped, but she was not subdued, and continued to denounce the overseer and to pour upon him every vile epithet of which she could think. Such floggings are seldom repeated on the same persons by overseers. They prefer to whip those who are most easily whipped. The doctrine that submission to violence is the best cure for violence did not hold good as between slaves and overseers. He was whipped oftener who was whipped easiest. That slave who had the courage to stand up for himself against the overseer, although he might have many hard stripes at first, became while legally a slave virtually a freeman. "You can shoot me," said a slave to Rigby Hopkins, "but you can't whip me," and the result was he was neither whipped nor shot.

Our Heads Are in the Lion's Mouth (1862)*

John S. Rock

In January, 1862, Negro abolitionist leader John S. Rock delivered the following speech to the Massachusetts Anti-Slavery Society. The Civil War was then entering its second year and another year would pass before President Lincoln issued his Proclamation emancipating the slaves in rebel areas. Rock here expresses the chagrin of northern Negroes at the reluctance of the federal government to move against slavery and at the continued manifestations of race prejudice in the North.

Ladies and Gentlemen:

I am here not so much to make a speech as to add a little more *color* to this occasion.

I do not know that it is right that I should speak, at this time, for it is said that we have talked too much already; and it is being continually thundered in our ears that the time for speech-making has ended, and the time for action has arrived. Perhaps this is so. This may be the theory of the people, but we all know that the active idea has found but little sympathy with either of our great military commanders, or the national executive; for they have told us, again and again, that "patience is a cure for all sores," and that we must wait for the good time which, to us, has been long a-coming.

It is not my desire, neither is it the time for me to criticize the government, even if I had the disposition so to do. The situation of the Black man in this country is far from being an enviable one. Today, our heads are in the lion's mouth, and we must get them out

---

* From the speech of John S. Rock, Annual Meeting of the Massachusetts Anti-Slavery Society, January 23, 1862, in *The Liberator* (February 14, 1862).

the best way we can. To contend against the government is as difficult as it is to sit in Rome and fight with the Pope. It is probable
that if we had the malice of the Anglo-Saxon we would watch our
chances and seize the first opportunity to take our revenge. If we
attempted this, the odds would be against us, and the first thing we
should know would be—nothing! The most of us are capable of
perceiving that the man who spits against the wind, spits in his
own face! . . .

This nation is mad. In its devoted attachment to the Negro, it
has run crazy after him, and now, having caught him, hangs on
with a deadly grasp and says to him, with more earnestness and
pathos than Ruth expressed to Naomi, "Whither thou goest, I will
go; where thou lodgest, I will lodge; thy people shall be my people,
and thy God, my God." . . .

The educated and wealthy class despise the Negro, because they
have robbed him of his hard earnings, or at least have got rich off
the fruits of his labor; and they believe if he gets his freedom their
fountain will be dried up and they will be obliged to seek business
in a new channel. Their "occupation will be gone." The lowest class
hate him because he is poor, as they are, and he is a competitor with
them for the same labor. The poor ignorant White man, who does
not understand that the interest of the laboring classes is mutual,
argues in this wise: "Here is so much labor to be performed—that
Negro does it. If he was gone, I should have his place." . . . I am
happy to state that there are many who have never known this sin,
and many others who have been converted to the truth by the
"foolishness of antislavery preaching," and are deeply interested
in the welfare of the race, and never hesitate to use their means
and their influence to help break off the yoke that has been so long
crushing us. I thank them all, and hope the number may be multi-
plied, until we shall have a people who will know no man save by his
virtues and his merits.

Now it seems to me that a blind man can see that the present
war is an effort to nationalize, perpetuate, and extend slavery in
this country. In short, slavery is the cause of the war: I might say,
is *the* war itself. Had it not been for slavery, we should have had no
war! Through 240 years of indescribable tortures, slavery has
wrung out of the blood, bones, and muscles of the Negro hundreds
of millions of dollars, and helped much to make this nation rich.

At the same time, it has developed a volcano which has burst forth, and, in a less number of days than years, has dissipated this wealth and rendered the government bankrupt! And, strange as it may appear, you still cling to this monstrous iniquity notwithstanding it is daily sinking the country lower and lower! Some of our ablest and best men have been sacrificed to appease the wrath of this American god.

The government wishes to bring back the country to what it was before. This is possible; but what is to be gained by it? If we are fools enough to retain the cancer that is eating out our vitals, when we can safely extirpate it, who will pity us if we see our mistake when we are past recovery? The abolitionists saw this day of tribulation and reign of terror long ago, and warned you of it; *but you would not hear!* You now say that it is their agitation, which has brought about this terrible civil war! That is to say, your friend sees a slow match set near a keg of gunpowder in your house and timely warns you of the danger which he sees is inevitable; you despise his warning, and after the explosion say [that] if he had not told you of it it would not have happened!

Now, when some leading men who hold with the policy of the President, and yet pretend to be liberal, argue that while they are willing to admit that the slave has an undoubted right to his liberty, the master has an equal right to his property; that to liberate the slave would be to injure the master, and a greater good would be accomplished to the country in these times by the loyal master's retaining his property than by giving to the slave his liberty—I do not understand it so. Slavery is treason against God, man, and the nation. The master has no right to be a partner in a conspiracy which has shaken the very foundation of the government. Even to apologize for it, while in open rebellion, is to aid and abet in treason. The master's right to his property in human flesh cannot be equal to the slave's right to his liberty.

Today, when it is a military necessity, and when the safety of the country is dependent upon emancipation, our humane political philosophers are puzzled to know what would become of the slaves if they were emancipated! The idea seems to prevail that the poor things would suffer, if robbed of the glorious privileges they now enjoy! If they could not be flogged, half-starved, and work to support in ease and luxury those who have never waived an opportunity to outrage and wrong them, they would pine away and die! Do you imagine that the Negro can live outside of slavery? Of course, now, they can take care of themselves and their masters too; but if you give them their liberty, must they not suffer? Have you never been able to see through all this? Have you not observed that the location of this organ of sympathy is in the pocket of the slaveholder and the man who shares in the profits of slave labor? Of course you have; and pity those men who have lived upon their ill-gotten wealth. You know, if they do not have somebody to work for them, they must leave their gilded salons, and take off their coats and roll up their sleeves, and take their chances among the *live* men of the world. This, you are aware, these respectable gentlemen will not do, for they have been so long accustomed to live by robbing and cheating the Negro that they are sworn never to work while they can live by plunder.

Can the slaves take care of themselves? What do you suppose becomes of the thousands who fly ragged and penniless from the South every year, and scatter themselves throughout the free states of the North? Do they take care of themselves? I am neither ashamed nor afraid to meet this question. Assertions like this, long contradicted, seem to be admitted as established facts. I ask your attention for one moment to the fact that Colored men in the North are shut out of almost every avenue to wealth, and yet, strange to say, the proportion of paupers is much less among us than among you! Are the beggars in the streets of Boston Colored men? In Philadelphia, where there is a larger free Colored population than is to be found in any other city in the free states, and where we are denied every social privilege, and are not even permitted to send our children to the schools that we are taxed to support, or to ride in the city horse cars, yet even there we pay taxes enough to support our own poor, and have a balance of a few thousand in our favor, which goes to support those "poor Whites" who "can't take care of themselves."

Many of those who advocate emancipation as a military necessity seem puzzled to know what is best to be done with the slave, if he is set at liberty. Colonization in Africa, Haiti, Florida, and South America are favorite theories with many well-informed persons. This is really interesting! No wonder Europe does not sympathize with you. You are the only people, claiming to be civilized, who take away the rights of those whose color differs from your own. If you find that you cannot rob the Negro of his labor and of himself, you will banish him! What a sublime idea! You are certainly a great people! What is your plea? Why, that the slaveholders will not permit us to live among them as freemen, and that the air of northern latitudes is not good for us! Let me tell you, my friends, *the slaveholders are not the men we dread!* They do not desire to have us removed. The northern proslavery men have done the free people of color tenfold more injury than the southern slaveholders. In the South, it is simply a question of dollars and cents. The slaveholder cares no more for you than he does for me. They enslave their own children, and sell them, and they would as soon enslave White men as Black men. The secret of the slaveholder's attachment to slavery is to be found in the dollar, and *that* he is determined to get without working for it. There is no prejudice against color among the slaveholders. Their social system and one million of mulattoes are facts which no arguments can demolish. If the slaves were emancipated, they would remain where they are. Black labor in the South is at a premium. The free man of color there has always had the preference over the White laborer. Many of you are aware that southerners will do a favor for a free Colored man, when they will not do it for a White man in the same condition in life. They believe in their institution because it supports them. . . .

When the orange is squeezed, we throw it aside. The Black man is a good fellow while he is a slave, and toils for nothing, but the moment he claims his own flesh and blood and bones, he is a most obnoxious creature, and there is a proposition to get rid of him! He is happy while he remains a poor, degraded, ignorant slave, without even the right to his own offspring. While [he is] in this condition, [his] master can ride in the same carriage, sleep in the same bed, and nurse from the same bosom. But give this same slave the right to use his own legs, his hands, his body, and his mind, and this happy and desirable creature is instantly transformed into a miserable and loathsome wretch, fit only to be colonized somewhere near the mountains of the moon, or eternally banished from the presence of all civilized beings. You must not lose sight of the fact that it is the emancipated slave and the free Colored man whom it is proposed to remove—not the slave: this country and climate are perfectly adapted to Negro slavery; it is the free Black that the air is not good for! What an idea! A country good for slavery, and not good for freedom! . . .

Not Benevolence but Simply Justice (1865)*

Frederick Douglass

During the Reconstruction Era that followed the Civil War the efforts of equal-rights advocates, the intransigent attitude of the defeated South and the political needs of northern Republicans all briefly combined to effect a national commitment to the principle of full equality for all Americans before the law, irrespective of race, color, or creed. That commitment, however, lasted less than a dozen years. Thereafter, racial violence in the South and de facto discrimination in the North emasculated the Fourteenth and Fifteenth Amendments to the Constitution, the tangible fruits of Reconstruction. By the end of the nineteenth century color-caste had replaced slavery as the dominant factor shaping race relations in America. In the following speech, delivered in 1865, Frederick Douglass makes the case for full manhood suffrage for the emancipated slaves.

. . . What is freedom? It is the right to choose one's own employment. Certainly it means that, if it means anything. And when any individual or combination of individuals undertakes to decide for any man when he shall work, and where he shall work, at what he shall work, and for what he shall work, he or they practically reduce him to slavery. He is a slave. . . . It defeats the beneficent intentions of the government, if it has beneficent intentions, in regard to the freedom of our people.

I have had but one idea for the last three years to present to the American people, and the phraseology in which I clothe it is the old abolition phraseology. I am for the "immediate, unconditional, and

---

* Speech of Frederick Douglass, Annual Meeting of the Massachusetts Anti-Slavery Society, Boston, April, 1865, in William D. Kelley, *et al.*, *The Equality of All Men Before the Law Claimed and Defended in Speeches by Hon. William D. Kelley, Wendell Phillips, and Frederick Douglass* (Boston: Massachusetts Anti-Slavery Society, 1865), pp. 36–39.

universal" enfranchisement of the Black man, in every state in the Union. Without this, his liberty is mockery; without this, you might as well almost retain the old name of slavery for his condition; for, in fact, if he is not the slave of the individual master, he is the slave of society and holds his liberty as a privilege, not as a right. He is at the mercy of the mob, and has no means of protecting himself.

It may be objected, however, that this pressing of the Negro's right to suffrage is premature.

. . . .

It may be asked, "Why do you want it? Some men have got along very well without it. Women have not this right." Shall we justify one wrong by another? That is a sufficient answer. Shall we at this moment justify the deprivation of the Negro of the right to vote, because someone else is deprived of that privilege? We may be asked, I say, why we want it. I will tell you why we want it. We want it because it is our *right,* first of all. No class of men can, without insulting their own nature, be content with any deprivation of their rights. We want it, again, as a means for educating our race. Men are so constituted that they derive their conviction of their own possibilities largely from the estimate formed of them by others. If nothing is expected of a people, that people will find it difficult to contradict that expectation. By depriving us of suffrage, you affirm our incapacity to form an intelligent judgment respecting public men and public measures; you declare before the world that we are unfit to exercise the elective franchise, and by this means lead us to undervalue ourselves, to put a low estimate upon ourselves, and to feel that we have no possibilities like other men. Again, I want the elective franchise . . . because ours is a peculiar government, based upon a peculiar idea, and that idea is universal suffrage. If I were in a monarchial government, or an autocratic or aristocratic government, where the few bore rule and the many were subject, there would be no special stigma resting upon me because I did not exercise the elective franchise. It would do me no great violence. . . . But here, where universal suffrage is the rule, where that is the fundamental idea of the government, to rule us out is to make us an exception, to brand us with the stigma of inferiority, and to invite to our heads the missiles of those about us; therefore, I want the franchise for the Black man.

. . . .

I know that we are inferior to you in some things—virtually inferior. We walk about you like dwarfs among giants. Our heads are scarcely seen above the great sea of humanity. The Germans are superior to us; the Irish are superior to us; the Yankees are superior to us; they can do what we cannot, that is, what we have not hitherto been allowed to do. But while I make this admission, I utterly deny that we are originally, or naturally, or practically, or in any way, or in any important sense, inferior to anybody on this globe. This charge of inferiority is an old dodge. It has been made available for oppression on many occasions. It is only about six centuries since the blue-eyed and fair-haired Anglo-Saxons were considered inferior by the haughty Normans, who once trampled upon them. If you read the history of the Norman Conquest, you will find that this proud Anglo-Saxon was once looked upon as of coarser clay than his Norman master, and might be found in the highways and byways of old England laboring with a brass collar on his neck, and the name of his master marked upon it. *You* were down then! You are up now. I am glad you are up, and I want you to be glad to help us up also.

The story of our inferiority is an old dodge, as I have said; for wherever men oppress their fellows, wherever they enslave them, they will endeavor to find the needed apology for such enslavement and oppression in the character of the people oppressed and enslaved. . . . So, too, the Negro, when he is to be robbed of any right which is justly his, is an "inferior man." It is said that we are ignorant; I admit it. But if we know enough to be hung, we know enough to vote. If the Negro knows enough to pay taxes to support the government, he knows enough to vote; taxation and representation should go together. If he knows enough to shoulder a musket and fight for the flag, fight for the government, he knows enough to vote. . . .

I hold that the American government has taken upon itself a solemn obligation of honor, to see that this war—let it be long or let it be short, let it cost much or let it cost little—that this war shall not cease until every freedman in the South has the right to vote. It has bound itself to it. What have you asked the Black men of the South, the Black men of the whole country, to do? Why, you have asked them to incur the deadly enmity of their masters in order to befriend you and to befriend this government. . . . You have called upon us to turn our backs upon our masters, to abandon their cause and espouse yours; to turn against the South . . . in favor of the North; to shoot down the Confederacy and uphold the flag—the American flag. . . . And now, what do you propose to do when you come to make peace? To reward your enemies, and trample in the dust your friends? Do you intend to sacrifice the very men who have come to the rescue of your banner in the South, and incurred the lasting displeasure of their masters thereby? Do you intend to sacrifice them and reward your enemies? Do you mean to give your enemies the right to vote, and take it away from your friends? Is that wise policy? Is that honorable? Could American honor withstand such a blow? I do not believe you will do it. I think you will see to it that we have the right to vote. There is something too mean in looking upon the Negro, when you are in trouble, as a citizen, and when you are free from trouble, as an alien. When this nation was in trouble, in its early struggles, it looked upon the Negro as a citizen. In 1776 he was a citizen. At the time of the formation of the Constitution the Negro had the right to vote in eleven states out of the old thirteen. In your trouble you have made us citizens. In 1812 General [Andrew] Jackson addressed us as citizens— "fellow citizens." He wanted us to fight. We were citizens then! And now, when you come to frame a conscription bill, the Negro is a citizen again. He has been a citizen just three times in the history of this government, and it has always been in time of trouble. In time of trouble we are citizens. Shall we be citizens in war, and aliens in peace? Would that be just? . . . I think the American people are disposed often to be generous rather than just. I look over this country at the present time, and I see educational societies, sanitary commissions, freedmen's associations, and the like—all very good. But in regard to the Colored people there is always more that is benevolent, I perceive, than just, manifested towards us. What I ask for the Negro is not benevolence, not pity, not sympathy, but simply *justice*.

The American people have always been anxious to know what they shall do with us. . . . Everybody has asked the question, and they learned to ask it early of the abolitionists, "What shall we do with the Negro?" I have had but one answer from the beginning: Do nothing with us! . . . All I ask is, give him a chance to stand on his own legs! Let him alone! If you see him on his way to school, let him alone, don't disturb him! If you see him going to the ballotbox, let him alone, don't disturb him! If you see him going into a workshop, just let him alone—your interference is doing him a positive injury. . . . If you will only untie his hands, and give him a chance, I think he will live. He will work as readily for himself as the White man. A great many delusions have been swept away by this war. One was that the Negro would not work; he has proved his ability to work. Another was that the Negro would not fight, that he possessed only the most sheepish attributes of humanity, was a perfect lamb, or an "Uncle Tom" disposed to take off his coat whenever required, fold his hands, and be whipped by anybody who wanted to whip him. But the war has proved that there is a great deal of human nature in the Negro, and that "he will fight," as . . . our President said in earlier days than these, "when there is a reasonable probability of his whipping anybody."

Three Centuries of Discrimination (1947)*

W.E.B. Du Bois

In 1947 the executive officers of the National Association for the Advancement of Colored People presented an appeal for the redress of the grievances of the American Negro—not to the government of the United States, to which it had addressed innumerable such appeals—but to the Social Affairs Department of the newly formed United Nations. The following document, written by W.E.B. Du Bois, is an excerpt from the introduction to that appeal. Du Bois, veteran Negro activist, was born in Massachusetts in 1868. After a lifetime of struggle against racism in America, he repudiated his United States citizenship in 1961, applied for membership in the Communist Party and became a citizen of the new African nation of Ghana, where he died in 1963.

---

* W. E. Burghardt Du Bois, "Three Centuries of Discrimination," introduction to "A Statement on the Denial of Human Rights to Minorities in the Case of Citizens of Negro Descent in the United States of America and an Appeal to the United Nations for Redress," Presented to the Department of Social Affairs, United Nations, October 23, 1947; excerpts in *The Crisis* (December, 1947), 362–364, 379–381.

There were in the United States of America, 1940, 12,865,518 native-born citizens, something less than a tenth of the nation, who form largely a segregated caste, with restricted legal rights, and many illegal disabilities. They are descendants of the Africans brought to America during the sixteenth, seventeenth, eighteenth and nineteenth centuries and reduced to slave labor. This group has no complete biological unity, but varies in color from white to black, and comprises a great variety of physical characteristics, since many are the offspring of White European-Americans as well as of Africans and American Indians. There are a large number of White Americans who also descend from Negroes but who are not counted in the Colored group nor subjected to caste restrictions because the preponderance of White blood conceals their descent.

The so-called American Negro group, therefore, while it is in no sense absolutely set off physically from its fellow Americans has nevertheless a strong, hereditary cultural unity, born of slavery, of common suffering, prolonged proscription and curtailment of political and civil rights; and especially because of economic and social disabilities. Largely from this fact, have arisen their cultural gifts to America—their rhythm, music and folksong; their religious faith and customs; their contribution to American art and literature; their defense of their country in every war, on land, sea and in the air; and especially the hard, continuous toil upon which the prosperity and wealth of this continent has largely been built.

The group has long been internally divided by dilemma as to whether its striving upward should be aimed at strengthening its inner cultural and group bonds, both for intrinsic progress and for offensive power against caste; or whether it should seek escape wherever and however possible into the surrounding American culture. Decision in this matter has been largely determined by outer compulsion rather than inner plan; for prolonged policies of segregation and discrimination have involuntarily welded the mass almost into a nation within a nation with its own schools, churches, hospitals, newspapers and many business enterprises.

The result has been to make American Negroes to wide extent provincial, self-conscious, and narrowly race-loyal; but it has also inspired them to frantic and often successful effort to achieve, to deserve, to show the world their capacity to share modern civilization. As a result there is almost no area of American civilization in which the Negro has not made creditable showing in the face of all his handicaps.

If, however, the effect of the color-caste system on the North American Negro has been good and bad, its effect on White America has been disastrous. It has repeatedly led the greatest modern attempt at democratic government to deny its political ideals, to falsify its philanthropic assertions and to make its religion to a great extent hypocritical. A nation which boldly declared "that all men are created equal," proceeded to build its economy on chattel slavery; masters who declared race-mixture impossible, sold their own children into slavery and left a mulatto progeny which neither law nor science can today disentagle; churches which excused slavery as calling the heathen to God, refused to recognize the freedom of converts or admit them to equal communion. Sectional strife over the profits of slave labor and conscientious revolt against making human beings real estate led to bloody civil war, and to a partial emancipation of slaves which nevertheless even to this day is not complete. Poverty, ignorance, disease, and crime have been forced on these unfortunate victims of greed to an extent far beyond any social necessity; and a great nation, which today ought to be in the forefront of the march toward peace and democracy, finds itself continuously making common cause with race-hate, prejudiced exploitation and oppression of the common man. Its high and noble words are turned against it, because they are contradicted in every syllable by the treatment of the American Negro for 328 years.

Slavery in America is a strange and contradictory story. It cannot be regarded as mainly either a theoretical problem of morals or a scientific problem of race. From either of these points of view, the rise of slavery in America is simply inexplicable. Looking at the facts frankly, slavery evidently was a matter of economics, a question of income and labor, rather than a problem of right and wrong, or of the physical differences in men. Once slavery began to be the source of vast income for men and nations, there followed frantic search for moral and racial justifications. Such excuses were found and men did not inquire too carefully into either their logic or truth.

The twenty Negroes brought to Virginia in 1619 were not the first who had landed on this continent. For a century small numbers of Negroes had been arriving as servants, as laborers, as free adventurers. The southwestern part of the present United States was first traversed by four explorers of whom one was an African Negro. Negroes accompanied early explorers like D'Ayllon and Menendez in the southwestern United States. But just as the earlier Black visitors to the West Indies were servants and adventurers and then later began to appear as laborers on the sugar plantations, so in Virginia, these imported Black laborers in 1619 and after, came to be wanted for the raising of tobacco which was the money crop.

In the minds of the early planters, there was no distinction as to labor whether it was White or Black; in law there was at first no discrimination. But as imported White labor became scarcer and scarcer and more protected by law, it became less profitable than Negro labor which flooded the markets because of European slave traders, internal strife in Africa and because in America the Negroes were increasingly stripped of legal defense. For these reasons America became a land of Black slavery, and there arose first the fabulously rich sugar empire then the cotton kingdom, and finally colonial imperialism.

Then came the inevitable fight between free labor and democracy on the one hand, and slave labor with its huge profits on the other. Black slaves were the spearhead of this fight. They were the first in America to stage the "sit-down" strike, to slow up and sabotage the work of the plantation. They revolted time after time and no matter what recorded history may say, the enacted laws against slave revolt are unanswerable testimony as to what these revolts meant all over America.

The slaves themselves especially imperiled the whole slave system by escape from slavery. It was the fugitive slave more than the slave revolt which finally threatened investment and income; and the organization for helping fugitive slaves through free northern Negroes and their White friends, in the guise of an underground movement, was of tremendous influence.

Finally it was the Negro soldier as a cofighter with the Whites for independence from the British economic empire which began emancipation. The British bid for his help and the colonials against their first impulse had to bid in return and virtually to promise the Negro soldier freedom after the Revolutionary War. It was for the protection of American Negro sailors as well as Whites that the war of 1812 was precipitated and, after independence from England was accomplished, freedom for the Black laboring class and enfranchisement for Whites and Blacks was in sight.

In the meantime, however, White labor had continued to regard the United States as a place of refuge; as a place for free land; for continuous employment and high wage; for freedom of thought and faith. It was here, however, that employers intervened; not because of any moral obliquity but because the industrial revolution, based on the crops raised by slave labor in the Caribbean and in the southern United States, was made possible by world trade and a new and astonishing technique; and finally was made triumphant by a vast transportation of slave labor through the British slave trade in the eighteenth and early nineteenth centuries.

This new mass of slaves became competitors of White labor and drove White labor for refuge into the arms of employers, whose interests were founded on slave labor. The doctrine of race infeririority was used to convince White labor that they had the right to be free and to vote, while the Negroes must be slaves or depress the wage of Whites; western free soil became additional lure and compensation, if it could be restricted to free labor.

On the other hand the fight of the slaveholders against democracy increased with the spread of the wealth and power of the Cotton Kingdom. Through political power based on slaves they became the dominant political force in the United States; they were successful in expanding into Mexico and tried to penetrate the Caribbean. Finally they demanded for slavery a part of the free soil of the West, and because of this last excessive, and in fact impossible, effort a Civil War to preserve and extend slavery ensued.

This fight for slave labor was echoed in the law. The free Negro was systematically discouraged, disfranchised and reduced to serfdom. He became by law the easy victim of the kidnapper and liable to treatment as a fugitive slave. The Church, influenced by wealth and respectability, was predominantly on the side of the slaveowner and effort was made to make the degradation of the Negro, as a race, final by Supreme Court decision.

But from the beginning, the outcome of the Civil War was inevitable and this mainly on account of the predominant wealth and power of the North; it was because of the clear fact that the southern slave economy was built on Black labor. If at any time the slaves or any large part of them, as workers, ceased to support the

South; and if even more decisively, as fighters, they joined the North, there was no way in the world for the South to win. Just as soon then as slaves became spies for the invading northern armies; laborers for their camps and fortifications; and finally produced 200,000 trained and efficient soldiers with arms in their hands, and with the possibility of a million more, the fate of the slave South was sealed.

Victory, however, brought dilemma; if victory meant full economic freedom for labor in the South, White and Black; if it meant land and education, and eventually votes; then the slave empire was doomed, and the profits of northern industry built on the southern slave foundation would also be seriously curtailed. Northern industry had a stake in the Cotton Kingdom and in the cheap slave labor that supported it. It had expanded for war industries during the fighting, encouraged by government subsidy and eventually protected by a huge tariff rampart. When war profits declined there was still prospect of tremendous postwar profits on cotton and other products of southern agriculture. Therefore, what the North wanted was not freedom and higher wages for Black Labor, but its control under such forms of law as would keep it cheap and also stop its open competition with northern labor. The moral protest of abolitionists must be appeased but profitable industry was determined to control wages and government.

The result was an attempt at Reconstruction in which Black labor established the schools; tried to divide up the land and put a new social legislation in force. On the other hand, the power of southern landowners soon joined with northern industry to disfranchise the Negro; keep him from access to free land or to capital, and to build up the present caste system for Blacks founded on color discrimination, peonage, intimidation, and mob violence.

It is this fact that underlies many of the contradictions in the social and political development of the United States since the Civil War. Despite our miraculous technique; despite comparatively high wage paid many of our workers and their consequent high standard of living; we are nevertheless ruled by wealth, monopoly and big-business organization to an astounding degree. Our railway transportation is built upon monumental economic injustice both to passengers, shippers, and to different sections of the land. The monopoly of land and natural resources throughout the United States, both in cities and in farming districts, is a disgraceful aftermath to the vast land heritage with which this nation started.

In 1876 the democratic process of government was crippled throughout the whole nation. This came about not simply through the disfranchisement of Negroes but through the fact that the political power of the disfranchised Negroes and of a large number of equally disfranchised Whites was preserved as the basis of political power, but the wielding of that power was left in the hands and under the control of the successors to the planter dynasty in the South.

Let us examine these facts more carefully. The United States has always professed to be a democracy. She has never wholly attained her ideal, but slowly she has approached it. The privilege of voting has in time been widened by abolishing limitations of birth, religion, and lack of property. After the Civil War, which abolished slavery, the nation in gratitude to the Black soldiers and laborers who helped win that war sought to admit to the suffrage all persons without distinction of "race, color or previous condition of servitude." They were warned by the great leaders of abolition, like [Charles] Sumner, [Thaddeus] Stevens and [Frederick A.] Douglass, that this could only be effective if the freedmen were given schools, land, and some minimum of capital. A Freedmen's Bureau to furnish these prerequisites to effective citizenship was planned and put into partial operation. But Congress and the nation, weary of the costs of war and eager to get back to profitable industry, refused the necessary funds. The effort died, but in order to restore friendly civil government in the South the enfranchised freedman, 75 per cent illiterate, without land or tools, was thrown into a competitive industry with a ballot in his hands. By herculean effort, helped by philanthropy and his own hard work, the Negro built a school system, bought land, and cooperated in starting a new economic order in the South. In a generation he had reduced his illiteracy by half and had become a wage-earning laborer and sharecropper. He still was handicapped by poverty, disease, and crime, but nevertheless the rise of the American Negro from slavery in 1860 to freedom in 1880 has few parallels in modern history.

However, opposition to any democracy which included the Negro race on any terms was so strong in the former slaveholding South, and found so much sympathy in large parts of the rest of the nation, that despite notable improvement in the condition of the Negro by every standard of social measurement, the effort to deprive Negroes of the right to vote succeeded. At first he was driven from the polls in the South by mobs and violence; and then he was openly cheated; finally by a "gentleman's agreement" with the North, the Negro was disfranchised in the South by a series of laws, methods of administration, court decisions, and general public policy, so that today three-fourths of the Negro population of the nation is deprived of the right to vote by open and declared policy.

Most persons seem to regard this as simply unfortunate for Negroes, as depriving a modern working class of the minimum rights for self-protection and opportunity for progress. This is true as has been shown in poor educational opportunities, discrimination in work, health protection, and in the courts. But the situation is far more serious than this: the disfranchisement of the American Negro makes the functioning of all democracy in the nation difficult; and as democracy fails to function in the leading democracy in the world, it fails in the world. . . .

This paradox and contradiction enters into our actions, thoughts and plans. After the First World War, we were alienated from the proposed League of Nations because of sympathy for imperialism and because of race antipathy to Japan and because we objected to the compulsory protection of minorities in Europe, which might lead to similar demands upon the United States. We joined Great Britain in determined refusal to recognize equality of races and nations; our tendency was toward isolation until we saw a chance to make inflated profits from the want which came upon the world. This effort of America to make profit out of the disaster in Europe was one of the causes of the depression of the thirties. . . .

But today the paradox again looms after the Second World War. We have recrudescence of race hate and caste restrictions in the United States and of these dangerous tendencies not simply for the United States itself but for all nations. When will nations learn that their enemies are quite as often within their own country as without? It is not Russia that threatens the United States so much as Mississippi; not Stalin and Molotov but Bilbo and Rankin*; internal injustice done to one's brothers is far more dangerous than the aggression of strangers from abroad.

Finally it must be stressed that the discrimination of which we complain is not simply discrimination against poverty and ignorance, which the world by long custom is used to see; the discrimination practiced in the United States is practiced against American Negroes in spite of wealth, training, and character. One of the contributors of this statement happens to be a White man but the other three and the editor himself are subject to Jim Crow laws, to denial of the right to vote, to inequal chance to earn a living; of the right to enter many places of public entertainment supported by their taxes. In other words our complaint is mainly a discrimination based mainly on color of skin, and it is this that we denounce as not only indefensible but barbaric. . . .

---

* Theodore Bilbo (1877–1947) was elected senator from Mississippi in 1935. In 1947 he was censored by a Senate committee for breaking federal laws in his dealings with war contractors and was investigated on charges of working to prevent Negroes from voting. Jeannette Rankin was the first woman elected to Congress. She voted against the nation's entry into both world wars.

Chapter Two

Radical Alternatives to Integration in the Nineteenth Century

The belief that evolutionary progress towards racial integration and the perfection of the American creed would eventually eliminate the exploitation and degradation that has been the Black man's historic lot in America has always been rejected by more radical Negro leaders. Their ideas have been less congenial to the dominant White population than those of the spokesmen for the integrationist or accommodationist programs and have therefore been less widely publicized. The radical strains of Negro protest thought have, however, had a strong appeal to large segments of the Negro community; they form an important part of the intellectual heritage of the modern Black Power movement. The documents in this chapter are drawn from the speeches and writings of nineteenth century advocates of revolutionary and separatist ideas.

The nineteenth century Black radicals, wrote W. E. B. Du Bois at the turn of the century,

> represented the attitude of revolt and revenge; they hate the White South blindly and distrust the White race generally, and so far as they agree on definite action, think that the Negro's only hope lies in emigration beyond the borders of the United States.*

---

* W.E.B. Du Bois, *The Souls of Black Folk* (Chicago: A. C. McClurg and Company, 1903), p. 52.

In the early nineteenth century, they advocated violent resistance to the slave system and gloried in the history of slave revolts in America and abroad. Disillusioned by attempts to end or ameliorate slavery within the American constitutional framework and angered at the legal and extralegal discrimination that free Negroes faced in the free states, the radicals argued that the Black man would never find justice in America. They advocated emigration to Africa, to Haiti, or to a new Black Nation to be founded elsewhere. Although the American Colonization Society was organized by prominent White leaders more interested in removing the despised free Negro population than in abolishing slavery, many Negro radicals cooperated with it. Their efforts helped to encourage the emigration of several thousand American exslaves and free Negroes to Africa, where they founded the independent nation of Liberia.

Racial sentiments abated during the Civil War and the Reconstruction Era when the Emancipation Proclamation and the passage of the Thirteenth, Fourteenth, and Fifteenth Amendments to the Constitution encouraged fresh optimism about the promise of American life. Many of the Black radicals fought with the victorious Union army and participated vigorously in the attempt to rebuild the southern states on the basis of racial equality.

But the Reconstruction years, their hopes unfulfilled and their promises betrayed, were followed by a period of bitterness and frustration that endured throughout the remainder of the century. The South, freed from federal interference by a lasting compromise between conservative northern economic interests and southern racists, ruthlessly exploited its Negro population economically and gradually erected an ironclad edifice of legal discrimination and segregation. The Jim Crow system, designed to reduce the Black man to a permanently debased peasant status, was perfected in the 1890's during an unprecedentedly virulent campaign of racist propaganda and violence.* In the northern states during the same period, the emergence of imperialist sentiment and activities, usually directed at non-White people, gave great prominence to racist doctrines. The Supreme Court, in important decisions in 1883 and 1896, sanctioned the segregation codes.†

Against that background, radical and separatist ideas again gained wide currency in the Negro community. Their advocates achieved little organizational success before the turn of the century, but they laid a firm foundation for the emergence and proliferation of Black Nationalist ideologies in the twentieth century.**

---

* C. Vann Woodward, *The Strange Career of Jim Crow* (New York: Galaxy Press, 1965).

† Rayford W. Logan, *The Negro in American Life and Thought: 1877 to 1901* (New York: Van Nostrand, 1954).

** August Meier, *Negro Thought in America, 1880–1915* (Ann Arbor: University of Michigan Press, 1963).

The Fourth of July Is an Insult (1857)*

Charles Lennox Redmond

Although Negro slavery was not mentioned directly in the original United States Constitution, clauses allowing a state to count three-fifths of its bound population for determining representation in Congress and providing for the return of fugitives gave it implicit recognition. In 1857, the Supreme Court, in the Dred Scott decision, declared that no Negro, slave or free, could claim constitutional rights in the United States. In the following document, Charles Lenox Redmond, a prominent Negro abolitionist, argued that no Black man could feel allegiance to the United States.

Mr. President, and Ladies and Gentlemen:

I hardly need inform those who are gathered together here to-day that I take some satisfaction in responding to the kind invitation of the Committee of the Massachusetts Anti-Slavery Society, for more reasons, perhaps, than would at first appear to many who are present. We have been informed, by the geneleman who preceded our respected President [Mr. Jackson], that this is a repetition of eighty years' standing of the demonstration of the American people on the side of liberty and independence. The reason why I above all others take pleasure in coming to this platform . . . is that I may have the satisfaction of saying, in a word, that I hold all demonstrations on this day, outside of the gatherings similar to the one of which we form a part, as so many mockeries and insults to a large number of our fellow-countrymen. Today there are, on the southern plantations, between three and four million to whom the popular Fourth of July in the United States of America is a most palpable insult; and to every White American who has any sympathy whatever with the oppressed, the day is also a mockery. Why, Sir, I have been informed since I came into this grove that on this platform sit one or two men recently from Virginia, known and owned there as slaves. I ask you, Mr. Chairman, and I ask this audience: What must be the emotions of these men who are now on their way from Virginia through the free state of Massachusetts

---

* From Charles Lenox Redmond, "An Anti-Slavery Discourse," *The Liberator* (July 10, 1857).

to Canada, where alone they can be free, happy, or out of danger?
I ask you if I say too much when I say that to the slave the popular
Fourth of July in the United States is an insult? . . . The time is
coming when a larger number than is gathered here today will sub-
scribe to the idea of the dissolution of the Union as the only means
of their own safety, as well as of the emancipation of the slave.

Sir, I do not care, so far as I am concerned, to view even the
deeds committed by the greatest men of the Revolution, nor the
purposes which they achieved. . . . I do know, in my heart, that
every slave on every plantation has the right from his God and
Creator to be free, and that is enough to warrant me in saying that
we cannot come here for a better or a nobler purpose than to help
forward the effort to dissolve the American Union; because if the
Union shall be dissolved, if for no other purpose than for the emancipation of the slave, it will be glory enough for me to engage in it.

I . . . speak for myself; and in doing so, I speak and determine
for the freedom of every slave on every plantation, and for the fugitives on my right hand; and in so speaking I speak for those before
me as emphatically as I can for the blackest man that lives or
suffers in our country. . . . I have not a word to say about the evils
of American slavery as they are detailed on the one hand, and re-
tailed on the other. The time has come for us to make the ground
upon which we stand today sacred to the cause of liberty; and when
we make the ground of Framingham thus sacred, we do away with
the necessity for the disgraceful underground railroad of our country that transports such men as these fugitives to the dominions
of the British Queen in order that they may secure their inalien-
able rights; we do away with the dishonor that now gathers around
and over the state of Massachusetts which makes it necessary for
any man or any woman to pass beyond our border before he or she
can be free. Talk to me of Bunker Hill, and tell me that a fugitive
passed through Boston today! Talk about Lexington, and tell me a
slave mother must be kept secreted in Boston! Talk to me of com-
memorating the memory of Joseph Warren, while 30,000 fugitive
slaves are in Canada! I will scout the memory of the Revolution,
the memory of Washington, and Adams, and Hancock, until the
soil of Massachusetts shall be as free to every fugitive, and as free
to me, as it is to the descendants of any one of them. And until we
shall do this, we talk in vain, and celebrate in vain.

O, Sir, I long to see the day when Massachusetts, and every New England state, shall be the only Canada needful to the American slave. I see Charles Sumner, on the one hand, in Europe trying to recover from illness and physical prostration, the result of American slavery; on the other hand, I see Kansas prostrate and bleeding, the result of American slavery. Before me, I see Horace Greeley, kicked and cuffed in the city of Washington, as the result of slavery. I look at Massachusetts, and I see our state, as an entire state, silently acquiescing in the recent disgraceful decision given by Judge [Roger B.] Taney in the United States Supreme Court, whereby it declared [in the Dred Scott decision] that the Black man in the United States has no rights which the White man is bound to respect! Shame on Judge Taney! Shame on the United States Supreme Court! Shame on Massachusetts, that she does not vindicate herself from the insult cast upon her through my own body, and through the body of every Colored man in the state! My God and Creator has given me rights which you are much bound to respect as those of the whitest man among you, if I make the exhibition of manhood at Bunker Hill, and Lexington, and Concord, as I can well testify. But in view of the ingratitude of the American people, in view of the baseness of such men as Judge Taney, in view of the dough-faced character that degrades our state, I regret exceedingly that there is one single drop of blood in my own veins that mingles with the blood of the men who engaged in the strife on Bunker Hill and at Lexington. Better that any such man had folded his hands and crossed his knees during the American Revolution, if this is the reward we are to derive from such hypocrites, such cowards, such panders to American slavery, as Judge Taney and his cooperators.

Mr. Chairman, I will not dwell upon this theme. I am not the man to speak to a White audience on the Fourth of July. I am reminded by everything over me, beneath me, and all around me, of my shame and degradation; and I shall take my seat on this occasion by stating to every White man present, who does not feel that the time has come when the rights of the Colored man should be restored to him, that I am among the number who would embrace this day, this moment, to strike the last fetter from the limbs of the last slave, if it were in my power to do so, and leave the consequences to those at whose instigation it has been fastened upon them.

I look around the country, and behold one other demonstration, and with the mention of that, I shall take my seat. . . . The election of James Buchanan to the presidency has placed that question beyond doubt and cavil, and has determined that the American people, by an overwhelming majority, are on the side of slavery, with all its infernalism. Now, Sir, it belongs to the true friends who are present to go forward, determined that this state of things shall be altered; and it can only be altered by the largest application and the freest promulgation of the doctrine set forth by the American and Massachusetts Anti-Slavery Societies. I am glad, therefore, to utter my testimony from a platform where they are represented; and let me say, friends, whether you believe it or not, that if the cause of universal liberty shall ever be established in our country, within our day and generation, it can only be by the promulgation to the country of the most radical type of antislavery. . . .

If You Must Bleed, Let it Come All at Once (1843)*

Henry Highland Garnet

National conventions of free Negroes met annually in the 1840's and 1850's to protest slavery and consider methods of improving the situation of the race in general. At the 1843 convention, Rev. Henry Highland Garnet, minister of a White Presbyterian congregation in Troy, New York, caused heated debate with the following call for slave uprisings. The convention rejected a motion to endorse Garnet's address by one vote and approved a resolution expressing faith that "a righteous government" would eventually abolish slavery.

Brethren and Fellow Citizens:
Your brethren of the North, East, and West have been accustomed to meet together in national conventions, to sympathize with each other, and to weep over your unhappy condition. In these meet-

---

* From Henry Highland Garnet, "An Address to the Slaves of the United States of America," in Garnet, *A Memorial Discourse Delivered in the Hall of the House of Representatives* (Philadelphia: James M. Wilson Co., 1865), pp. 44-51.

ings we have addressed all classes of the free, but we have never, until this time, sent a word of consolation and advice to you. We have been contented in sitting still and mourning over your sorrows, earnestly hoping that before this day your sacred liberties would have been restored. But we have hoped in vain. Years have rolled on, and tens of thousands have been borne on streams of blood and tears to the shores of eternity. While you have been oppressed, we have also been partakers with you; nor can we be free while you are enslaved. We therefore write to you as being bound with you.

Many of you are bound to us, not only by the ties of common humanity, but we are connected by the more tender relations of parents, wives, husbands, and sisters, and friends. As such we most affectionately address you.

Slavery has fixed a deep gulf between you and us, and while it shuts out from you the relief and consolation which your friends would willingly render, it afflicts and persecutes you with a fierceness which we might not expect to see in the fiends of hell. But still the Almighty Father of mercies has left to us a glimmering ray of hope, which shines out like a lone star in a cloudy sky. Mankind are becoming wiser and better—the oppressor's power is fading and you, every day, are becoming better informed and more numerous. Your grievances, brethren, are many. We shall not attempt, in this short address, to present to the world all the dark catalogue of the nation's sins, which have been committed upon an innocent people. Nor is it indeed necessary, for you feel them from day to day, and all the civilized world looks upon them with amazement.

Two hundred and twenty-seven years ago the first of our injured race were brought to the shores of America. They came not with glad spirits to select their homes in the New World. They came not with their own consent, to find an unmolested enjoyment of the blessings of this fruitful soil. The first dealings they had with men calling themselves Christians exhibited to them the worst features of corrupt and sordid hearts and convinced them that no cruelty is too great, no villainy and no robbery too abhorrent, for even enlightened men to perform when influenced by avarice and lust. Neither did they come flying upon the wings of Liberty to a land of freedom. But they came with broken hearts, from their beloved native land, and were doomed to unrequited toil and deep degradation. Nor did the evil of their bondage end at their emancipation by death. Succeeding generations inherited their chains, and millions have come from eternity into time, and have returned again to the world of spirits, cursed and ruined by American slavery.

The propagators of the system, or their immediate successors, very soon discovered its growing evil, and its tremendous wickedness, and secret promises were made to destroy it. The gross inconsistency of a people holding slaves, who had themselves "ferried o'er the wave" for freedom's sake, was too apparent to be entirely overlooked. The voice of Freedom cried, "Emancipate your slaves." Humanity supplicated with tears for the deliverance of the children of Africa. Wisdom urged her solemn plea. The bleeding captive pled his innocence, and pointed to Christianity who stood weeping at the cross. Jehovah frowned upon the nefarious institution, and thunderbolts, red with vengeance, struggled to leap forth to blast the guilty wretches who maintained it. But all was in vain. Slavery had stretched its dark wings of death over the land, the Church stood silently by—the priests prophesied falsely, and the people loved to have it so. Its throne is established, and now it reigns triumphant.

Nearly three millions of your fellow citizens are prohibited by law and public opinion (which in this country is stronger than law) from reading the Book of Life. Your intellect has been destroyed as much as possible, and every ray of light they have attempted to shut out from your minds. The oppressors themselves have become involved in the ruin. They have become weak, sensual, and rapacious—they have cursed you—they have cursed themselves—they have cursed the earth which they have trod.

The colonies threw the blame upon England. They said that the mother country entailed the evil upon them, and they would rid themselves of it if they could. The world thought they were sincere, and the philanthropic pitied them. But time soon tested their sincerity. In a few years the colonists grew strong, and severed themselves from the British government. Their independence was declared, and they took their station among the sovereign powers of the earth. The declaration was a glorious document. Sages admired it, and the patriotic of every nation reverenced the godlike sentiments which it contained. When the power of government returned to their hands, did they emancipate their slaves? No, they rather added new links to our chains. Were they ignorant of the principles of Liberty? Certainly they were not. The sentiments of their revolutionary orators fell in burning eloquence upon their hearts, and with one voice they cried, "Liberty or Death." Oh, what a sentence was that! It ran from soul to soul like electric fire, and nerved the arms of thousands to fight in the holy cause of freedom. Among the diversity of opinions that are entertained in regard to physical resistance, there are but a few found to gainsay the stern declaration. We are among those who do not.

Slavery! How much misery is comprehended in that single word. What mind is there that does not shrink from its direful effects? Unless the image of God be obliterated from the soul, all men cherish the love of liberty. The nice discerning political economist does not regard the sacred right more than the untutored African who roams in the wilds of Congo. Nor has the one more right to full enjoyment of his freedom than the other. In every man's mind the good seeds of liberty are planted, and he who brings his fellow down so low, as to make him contented with a condition of slavery, commits the highest crime against God and man. Brethren, your oppressors aim to do this. They endeavor to make you as much like brutes as possible. When they have blinded the eyes of your mind —when they have embittered the sweet waters of life—when they have shut out the light which shines from the word of God—then, and not till then, has American slavery done its perfect work.

To such degradation it is sinful in the extreme for you to make voluntary submission. The divine commandments you are in duty bound to reverence and obey. If you do not obey them, you will surely meet with the displeasure of the Almighty. He requires you to love Him supremely, and your neighbor as yourself—to keep the Sabbath day holy—to search the Scriptures—and bring up your children with respect for His laws, and to worship no other God but Him. But slavery sets all these at nought, and hurls defiance in the face of Jehovah. The forlorn condition in which you are placed does not destroy your obligation to God. You are not certain of heaven because you allow yourselves to remain in a state of slavery. . . . God will not receive slavery, nor ignorance, nor any other state of mind, for love and obedience to Him. Your condition does not absolve you from your moral obligation. The diabolical injustice by which your liberties are cloven down, *neither God nor angels, or just men, command you to suffer for a single moment. Therefore it is your solemn and imperative duty to use every means, both moral, intellectual, and physical, that promises success.* If a band of heathen men should attempt to enslave a race of Christians, and to place their children under the influence of some false religion, surely Heaven would frown upon the men who would not resist such aggression, even to death. If, on the other hand, a band of Christians should attempt to enslave a race of heathen men, and to entail slavery upon them, and to keep them in heathenism in the midst of Christianity, the God of heaven would smile upon every effort which the injured might make to disenthral themselves.

Brethren, it is as wrong for your lordly oppressors to keep you in slavery as it was for the man-thief to steal our ancestors from the coast of Africa. You should therefore now use the same manner of resistance as would have been just in our ancestors when the bloody footprints of the first remorseless soul-thief was placed upon the shores of our fatherland. . . .

Brethren, the time has come when you must act for yourselves. It is an old and true saying that, "if hereditary bondsmen would be free, they must themselves strike the blow." You can plead your own cause and do the work of emancipation better than any others. The nations of the Old World are moving in the great cause of universal freedom, and some of them at least will, ere long, do you justice. The combined powers of Europe have placed their broad seal of disapprobation upon the African slave trade. But in the slaveholding parts of the United States the trade is as brisk as ever. They buy and sell you as though you were brute beasts. The North has done much—her opinion of slavery in the abstract is known. But in regard to the South, we adopt the opinion of the *New York Evangelist*—"We have advanced so far that the cause apparently waits for a more effectual door to be thrown open than has been yet." We are about to point you to that more effectual door. Look around you, and behold the bosoms of your loving wives heaving with untold agonies! Hear the cries of your poor children! Remember the stripes your fathers bore. Think of the torture and disgrace of your noble mothers. Think of your wretched sisters, loving virtue and purity, as they are driven into concubinage and are exposed to the unbridled lusts of incarnate devils. Think of the undying glory that hangs around the ancient name of Africa—and forget not that you are native-born American citizens, and as such you are justly entitled to all the rights that are granted to the freest. Think how many tears you have poured out upon the soil which you have cultivated with unrequited toil and enriched with your blood; and then go to your lordly enslavers and tell them plainly, that you *are determined to be free.* Appeal to their sense of justice, and tell them that they have no more right to oppress you than you have to enslave them. Entreat them to remove the grievous burdens which they have imposed upon you and to remunerate you for your labor. Promise them renewed diligence in the cultivation of the soil, if they will render to you an equivalent for your services. Point them to the increase of happiness and prosperity in the British West Indies since the Act of Emancipation. Tell them in language which they cannot misunderstand of the exceeding sinfulness of slavery, and of a future judgment, and of the righteous retributions of an indignant God. Inform them that all you desire is *freedom,* and that nothing else will suffice. Do this, and forever after cease to toil for the heartless tyrants, who give you no other reward but stripes and abuse. If they then commence work of death, they, and not you, will will be responsible for the consequences. You had far better all die—*die immediately*—than live slaves and entail your wretchedness upon your posterity. If you would be free in this generation, here is your only hope. However much you and all of us may desire it, there is not much hope of redemption without the shedding of blood. If you must bleed, let it all come at once—*rather die freemen than live to be the slaves.* It is impossible, like the children of Israel, to make a grand exodus from the land of bondage. The Pharaohs are on both sides of the blood-red waters! You cannot move *en masse* to the dominions of the British Queen—nor can you pass through Florida and overrun Texas, and at last find peace in Mexico. The propagators of American slavery are spending their blood and treasure that they may plant the black flag in the heart of Mexico and riot in the halls of Montezuma. In language of the Reverend Robert Hall, when addressing the volunteers of Bristol who were rushing forth to repel the invasion of Napoleon, who threatened to lay waste the fair homes of England, "Religion is too much interested in your behalf not to shed over you her most gracious influences."

You will not be compelled to spend much time in order to become inured to hardships. . . . Slavery has done this to make you subservient to its own purposes; but it has done more than this, it has prepared you for any emergency. If you receive good treatment, it is what you can hardly expect; if you meet with pain, sorrow, and even death, these are the common lot of the slaves.

Fellowmen! patient sufferers! behold your dearest rights crushed to the earth! See your sons murdered, and your wives, mothers, and sisters doomed to prostitution. In the name of the merciful God, and by all that life is worth, let it no longer be a debatable question, whether it is better to choose *liberty or death.*

In 1822, Denmark Veazie of South Carolina formed a plan for the liberation of his fellowmen. In the whole history of human efforts to overthrow slavery, a more complicated and tremendous plan was never formed. He was betrayed by the treachery of his own people, and died a martyr to freedom. Many a brave hero fell, but history, faithful to her high trust, will transcribe his name on the same monument with Moses, Hampden, Tell, Bruce and Wallace, Toussaint L'Ouverture, Lafayette, and Washington.* That tremendous movement shook the whole empire of slavery. The guilty soulthieves were overwhelmed with fear. It is a matter of fact that at this time, and in consequence of the threatened revolution, the slave States talked strongly of emancipation. But they blew but one blast of the trumpet of freedom, and then laid it aside. As these men became quiet, the slaveholders ceased to talk about emanipation; and now behold your condition today! Angels sigh over it, and humanity has long since exhausted her tears in weeping on your account!

---

* These men were all famous national leaders who have become legendary for their struggles to attain national independence. John Hampden (1594–1643) was a noted opponent of the Crown who raised a regiment of foot soldiers for the Parliamentary army during the English Civil War. William Tell is a legendary hero of Switzerland who represents the spirit of the Swiss movement for independence from the Austrian Hapsburgs during the twelfth century. Robert Bruce (1274–1329) was a Scottish king who defeated the English and gave Scotland its independence. William Wallace (1272–1305) was another Scottish patriot who led a band of guerrillas against the English armies. Toussaint L'Ouverture (1743–1803) was a former slave who liberated Haiti from French rule.

The patriotic Nathaniel Turner followed Denmark Veazie.* He was goaded to desperation by wrong and injustice. By despotism his name has been recorded on the list of infamy, and future generations will remember him among the noble and brave. Next arose the immortal Joseph Cinque, the hero of the Amistad. He was a native African, and by the help of God he emancipated a whole shipload of his fellowmen on the high seas. And he now sings of liberty on the sunny hills of Africa and beneath his native palm trees, where he hears the lion roar and feels himself as free as the king of the forest.

Next arose Madison Washington, that bright star of freedom, and took his station in the constellation of true heroism. He was a slave on board the brig *Creole,* of Richmond, bound to New Orleans, that great slave mart, with 104 others. Nineteen struck for liberty or death. But one life was taken, and the whole were emancipated, and the vessel was carried into Nassau, New Providence.

Noble men! Those who have fallen in freedom's conflict, their memories will be cherished by the true-hearted and the God-fearing in all future generations; those who are living, their names are surrounded by a halo of glory.

Brethren, arise, arise! Strike for your lives and liberties. Now is the day and the hour. Let every slave throughout the land do this, and the days of slavery are numbered. You cannot be more oppressed than you have been—you cannot suffer greater cruelties than you have already. *Rather die freemen than live to be slaves.* Remember that you are *four millions!*

. . . .

Let your motto be resistance! *resistance!* RESISTANCE! No oppressed people have ever secured their liberty without resistance. What kind of resistance you had better make you must decide by the circumstances that surround you, and according to the suggestion of expediency. Brethren, adieu! Trust in the living God. Labor for the peace of the human race, and remember that you are *four millions!*

---

* See succeeding article by William Wells Brown for more about Turner. Vesey (the more usual spelling) was to have led a revolt of Charleston slaves and freedmen, but his plot was discovered and foiled.

Every Eye Is Looking for Another Nat Turner (1863)*

William Wells Brown

William Wells Brown escaped from slavery in 1834. In 1853 he published the first novel written by an American Negro. Brown also wrote significant historical and biographical works. The following selection, taken from one of his histories, praises the memory of Nat Turner who led the largest and bloodiest of the American slave revolts, in 1832.

Reinforcements came to the Whites, and the Blacks were overpowered and defeated by the superior numbers of their enemy. In this battle many were slain on both sides. Will, the bloodthirsty and revengeful slave, fell with his broadaxe uplifted, after having laid three of the Whites dead at his feet with his own strong arm and his terrible weapon. His last words were, "Bury my axe with me." For he religiously believed that in the next world the Blacks would have a contest with the Whites, and that he would need his axe. Nat Turner, after fighting to the last with his short sword, escaped with some others to the woods near by, and was not captured for nearly two months. When brought to trial he pleaded "not guilty"; feeling, as he said, that it was always right for one to strike for his own liberty. After going through a mere form of trial, he was convicted and executed at Jerusalem, the county seat for Southampton County. Virginia. Not a limb trembled or a muscle was observed to move. Thus died Nat Turner, at the early age of thirty-one years — a martyr to the freedom of his race, and a victim to his own fanaticism. He meditated upon the wrongs of his oppressed and injured people, till the idea of their deliverance excluded all other ideas from his mind, and he devoted his life to its realization. Every thing appeared to him a vision, and all favorable omens were signs from God. That he was sincere in all that he professed there is not the slightest doubt. After being defeated he might have escaped to the free states, but the hope of raising a new band kept him from doing so.

---

* William Wells Brown, *The Black Man: His Antecedents, His Genius and His Achievements* (Savannah, Georgia: James M. Symmes & Co., 1863), pp. 70–75.

He impressed his image upon the minds of those who once beheld him. His looks, his sermons, his acts, and his heroism live in the hearts of his race, on every cotton, sugar, and rice plantation at the South. The present generation of slaves have a superstitious veneration for his name, and believe that in another insurrection Nat Turner will appear and take command. He foretold that at his death the sun would refuse to shine, and that there would be signs of disapprobation given from Heaven. And it is true that the sun was darkened, a storm gathered, and more boisterous weather had never appeared in Southampton County than on the day of Nat's execution. The sheriff, warned by the prisoner, refused to cut the cord that held the trap. No black man would touch the rope. A poor old White man, long besotted by drink, was brought forty miles to be the executioner. And even the planters, with all their prejudice and hatred, believed him [Turner] honest and sincere; for Mr. Gray, who had known Nat from boyhood, and to whom he made his confession, says of him—

It has been said that he was ignorant and cowardly, and that his object was to murder and rob, for the purpose of obtaining money to make his escape. It is notorious that he was never known to have a dollar in his life, to swear an oath, or drink a drop of spirits. As to his ignorance, he certainly never had the advantages of education; but he can read and write, and for natural intelligence and quickness of apprehension is surpassed by few men I have ever seen. As to his being a coward, his reason, as given, for not resisting Mr. Phipps, shows the decision of his character. When he saw Mr. Phipps present his gun, he said he knew it was impossible for him to escape, as the woods were full of men; he therefore thought it was better for him to surrender and trust to fortune for his escape. He is a complete fanatic, or plays his part most admirably. On other subjects he possesses an uncommon share of intelligence, with a mind capable of attaining anything but warped and perverted by the influence of early impressions. He is below the ordinary stature, though strong and active; having the true Negro face, every feature of which is strongly marked. I shall not attempt to describe the effect of his narrative, as told and commented on by himself, in the condemned hole of the prison; the calm, deliberate composure with which he spoke of his late deeds and intentions; the expressions of his fiendlike face when excited by enthusiasm—still bearing the stains of the blood of helpless innocence about him, clothed with rags and cov-

ered with chains, yet daring to raise his manacled hands to
heaven, with a spirit soaring above the attributes of man; I
looked on him, and the blood curdled in my veins.

Well might he feel the blood curdle in his veins, when he remembered that in every southern household there may be a Nat
Turner, in whose soul God has lighted a torch of liberty that cannot
be extinguished by the hand of man. The slaveholder should understand that he lives upon a volcano, which may burst forth at any
moment, and give freedom to his victims.

> Great God, hasten on the glad jubilee,
> When my brother in bonds shall arise and be free,
> And our blotted escutcheon be washed from its stains,
> Now the scorn of the world—four million in chains!
> O, then shall Columbia's proud flag be unfurled,
> The glory of freemen, and pride of the world,
> While earth's strolling millions point hither in glee,
> "To the land of the brave and the home of the free!"

Fifty-five Whites and seventy-three Blacks lost their lives in
the Southampton rebellion. On the fatal night when Nat and his
companions were dealing death to all they found, Captain Harris,
a wealthy planter, had his life saved by the devotion and timely
warning of his slave Jim, said to have been half-brother to his
master. After the revolt had been put down, and parties of Whites
were hunting the suspected Blacks, Captain Harris, with his faithful slave, went into the woods in search of the Negroes. In saving
his master's life, Jim felt that he had done his duty, and could not
consent to become a betrayer of his race, and, on reaching the
woods, he handed his pistol to his master, and said, "I cannot help
you hunt down these men; they, like myself, want to be free. Sir,
I am tired of the life of a slave; please give my freedom, or shoot
me on the spot." Captain Harris took the weapon and pointed it at
the slave. Jim, putting his right hand upon his heart, said, "This
is the spot; aim here." The captain fired, and the slave fell dead at
his feet.

From this insurrection and other manifestations of insubordi-
nation by the slave population, the southern people, if they are wise,
should learn a grave lesson; for the experience of the past might
give them some clue to the future.

Thirty years' free discussion has materially changed public opinion in the non-slaveholding states, and a Negro insurrection, in the present state of the nation, would not receive the condemnation that it did in 1831. The right of a man to the enjoyment of freedom is a settled point; and where he is deprived of this, without any criminal act of his own, it is his duty to regain his liberty at every cost.

If the oppressor is struck down in the contest, his fall will be a just one, and all the world will applaud the act.

This is a new era, and we are in the midst of the most important crisis that our country has yet witnessed. And in the crisis the Negro is an important item. Every eye is now turned towards the South, looking for another Nat Turner.

I Have No Hopes in This Country (1852)*

Martin R. Delaney

Martin Robison Delaney, a Harvard-educated physician, was the most prominent of the Black Zionists of the 1850's. Denying that Negroes could ever hope to receive full citizenship rights in the United States, Delaney promoted a variety of emigrationist schemes, some aimed at returning Negroes to Africa, others at establishing Black nations in the Caribbean or western Canada. He refused to cooperate with the American Colonization Society, denouncing its White leaders as "arrant hypocrites." In 1859 he led an expedition up the Niger River Valley and signed a treaty with the Yoruba tribe granting settlement rights to American Negroes. During the Civil War he served as a medical officer with the Union Army, attaining the rank of major.

Mr. Garrison
MY DEAR SIR:

.   .   .   .

I am not in favor of caste, nor a separation of the brotherhood of mankind, and would as willingly live among White men as Black

---

* Martin R. Delaney to William Lloyd Garrison, May 14, 1852; in *The Liberator* (May 21, 1852).

if I had an *equal possession and enjoyment* of privileges; but shall never be reconciled to live among them subservient to their will— existing by mere *sufferance* as we, the Colored people, do in this country. The majority of White men cannot see why Colored men cannot be satisfied with their condition in Massachusetts—what they desire more than the *granted* right of citizenship. Blind selfishness on the one hand and deep prejudice on the other, will not permit them to understand that we desire the *exercise* and *enjoyment* of these rights, as well as the *name* of their possession. If there were any probability of this, I should be willing to remain in the country, fighting and struggling on, the good fight of faith. But I must admit, that I have no hopes in this country—no confidence in the American people—with a *few* excellent exceptions—therefore, I have written as I have done. Heathenism and Liberty, before Christianity and Slavery.

> Were I a slave, I would be free
> I would not live to live a slave;
> But boldly *strike for* LIBERTY—
> For FREEDOM or a *Martyr's* grave.

Yours for God and Humanity,
M. R. DELANEY

Resolution of the Convention of Free Colored People (1852)*

The colonization movement made great gains during the late 1840's and 1850's as proslavery sentiment seemed to increase and as the condition of the free Negro population deteriorated. By the 1850's Negro emigrationist groups were holding their own national conventions.

WHEREAS, The present age is one distinguished for enquiry, investigation, enterprise and improvement in physical, political, intellectual, and moral sciences, we hold the truths to be self-evident

---

* From "Proceedings of the Convention of Free Colored People of the State of Maryland, Held in Baltimore, July 26, 27, 28, 1852," *Journal of Negro History, I* (July, 1916), 327–328.

that we are, as well as all mankind, created equal, and are endowed by our Creator with the right to enquire into our present condition and future prospects; and as a crisis has arisen in our history presenting a bright and glorious future, may we not hope that ere long the energies of our people may be aroused from their lethargy, and seek to obtain for themselves and posterity the rights and privileges of freemen—therefore,

Resolved: That while we appreciate and acknowledge the sincerity of the motives and the activity of the zeal of those who during an agitation of twenty years have honestly struggled to place us on a footing of social and political equality with the White population of this country, yet we cannot conceal from ourselves the fact that no advance has been made towards a result to us so desirable; but that on the contrary, our condition as a class is less desirable than it was twenty years ago.

Resolved: That in the face of an emigration from Europe which is greater each year than it was the year before, and during the prevalence of a feeling in regard to us which the very agitation intended for good has only served apparently to embitter, we cannot promise ourselves that the future will do that which the past has failed to accomplish.

Resolved: That recognising in ourselves the capacity to conduct honorably, and creditably, in public affairs; to acquire knowledge, and to enjoy the refinements of social intercourse; and having a praiseworthy ambition that this capacity should be developed to its full extent, we are naturally led to enquire where this can best be done, satisfied as we are that in this country, at all events from present appearances, it is out of the question.

Resolved: That in comparing the relative advantages of Canada, the West Indies and Liberia—these being the places beyond the limits of the United States to which circumstances have directed our attention—we are led to examine the claims of Liberia particularly, where alone we have been told that we can exercise all the functions of a free republican government and hold an honorable position among the nations of the earth.

Resolved: That in thus expressing our opinions it is not our purpose to counsel emigration as either necessary or proper in every case. The transfer of an entire people from one country to another must necessarily be the work of generations—each individual now and hereafter must be governed by the circumstances of his own condition, of which he alone can be the judge, as well in regard to the time of removal as to the place to which he shall remove; but deeply impressed ourselves with the conviction that sooner or later removal must take place, we would counsel our people to accustom themselves to the idea of it, and in suggesting Liberia to them we do so in the belief that it is there alone they can reasonably anticipate an independent national existence.

Resolved: That as this subject is one of greatest importance to us and the consideration of which, whatever may be the result, can not be put aside; we recommend to our people in this state to establish and maintain an organization in regard to it, the great object of which shall be enquiry and discussion, which without committing any one shall lead to accurate information; and that a convention like the present, composed of delegates from the counties and Baltimore city, be annually held at such time and place as said convention in their judgment may designate.

We Have No Wish to Separate from Our Present Homes (1836)*

James Forten

The colonization proposals generated a great deal of controversy within the American Negro community. In the following document, James Forten, who amassed a considerable fortune as a Philadelphia businessman, presents the point of view of those Negroes who eschewed emigration and preferred to believe that the wrongs of the Negro would be gradually righted by the march of progress. He delivered this address before the Ladies Anti-Slavery Society of Philadelphia on April 14, 1836.

The free people of color, assembled together under circumstances of deep interest to their happiness and welfare, humbly and

---

* James Forten, "An Address to the Humane and Benevolent Inhabitants of the City and County of Philadelphia," in Carter G. Woodson, *Negro Orators and Their Orations* (Washington, D.C.: Associated Publishers, Inc., 1925), pp. 52–55.

respectfully lay before you this expression of their feelings and apprehensions.

Relieved from the miseries of slavery, many of us by your aid, possessing the benefits which industry and integrity in this prosperous country assure to all its inhabitants, enjoying the rich blessings of religion, by opportunities of worshiping the only true God, under the light of Christianity, each of us according to his understanding; and having afforded to us and to our children the means of education and improvement; we have no wish to separate from our present homes, for any purpose whatever. Contented with our present situation and condition we are not desirous of increasing their prosperity, but by honest efforts and by the use of those opportunities for their improvement, which the Constitution and laws allow to all. It is therefore with painful solicitude, and sorrowing regret, we have seen a plan for colonizing the free people of color of the United States on the coast of Africa brought forward under the auspices and sanction of gentlemen whose names give value to all they recommend, and who certainly are among the wisest, the best, and the most benevolent of men in this great nation.

If the plan of colonizing is intended for our benefit and those who now promote it will never seek our injury we humbly and respectfully urge that it is not asked for by us; nor will it be required by any circumstances in our present or future condition as long as we shall be permitted to share the protection of the excellent laws and just government which we now enjoy, in common with every individual of the community.

We, therefore, a portion of those who are objects of this plan and among those whose happiness, with that of others of our color, it is intended to promote, with humble and grateful acknowledgements to those who have devised it, renounce and disclaim every connection with it and respectfully but firmly declare our determination not to participate in any part of it.

If this plan of colonization now proposed is intended to provide a refuge and a dwelling for a portion of our brethren who are now held in slavery in the South, we have other and stronger objections to it, and we entreat your consideration of them.

The ultimate and final abolition of slavery in the United States is, under the guidance and protection of a just God, progressing. Every year witnesses the release of numbers of the victims of oppression, and affords new and safe assurances that the freedom of all will in the end be accomplished. As they are thus by degrees relieved from bondage, our brethren have opportunities for instruction and improvement; and thus they become in some measure fitted for their liberty. Every year, many of us have restored to us by the gradual but certain march of the cause of abolition—parents, from whom we have been long separated—wives and children, whom we had left in servitude—and brothers, in blood as well as in early sufferings, from whom we had been long parted.

But if the emancipations of our kindred shall, when the plan of colonization shall go into effect, be attempted with transportation to a distant land and shall be granted on no other condition the consolation for our past sufferings and of those of our color who are in slavery, which has hitherto been and under the present situation of things would continue to be afforded to us and to them, will cease for ever. The cords which now connect them with us will be stretched by the distance to which their ends will be carried until they break; and all the sources of happiness, which affection and connection and blood bestow, will be ours or theirs no more.

Nor do we view the colonization of those who may become emancipated by its operation among our southern brethren as capable of producing their happiness. Unprepared by education and a knowledge of the truths of our blessed religion for their new situation, those who will thus become colonists will themselves be surrounded by every suffering which can afflict the members of the human family.

Without arts, without habits of industry, and unaccustomed to provide by their own exertions and foresight for their wants, the colony will soon become the abode of every vice and the home of every misery. Soon will the light of Christianity, which now dawns among that section of our species, be shut out by the clouds of ignorance, and their day of life be closed without the illuminations of the Gospel.

To those of our brethren who shall be left behind, there will be assured perpetual slavery and augmented sufferings. Diminished in numbers the slave population of the southern states, which by its magnitude alarms its proprietors, will be easily secured. . . . The southern masters will colonize only those whom it may be dangerous to keep among them. The bondage of a large portion of our brethren will thus be rendered perpetual.

Should the anticipations of misery and want among the colonists . . . be realized; to emancipate and transport to the colony will be held forth by slaveholders as the worst and heaviest of punishments, and they will be threatened and successfully used to enforce increased submission to their wishes and subjection to their commands.

Nor ought the sufferings and sorrows which must be produced by an exercise of the right to transport and colonize such only of their slaves as may be selected by the slaveholders escape the attention and consideration of those whom with all humility we now address. Parents will be torn from their children—husbands from their wives—brothers from brothers—and all the heart-rending agonies which were endured by our forefathers when they were dragged into bondage from Africa will be again renewed, and with increased anguish. The shores of America will like the sands of Africa be watered by the tears of those who will be left behind. Those who shall be carried away will roam childless, widowed, and alone, over the burning plains of Guinea.

Disclaiming, as we emphatically do, a wish or desire to interpose our opinions and feelings between all plans of colonization and the judgment of those whose wisdom as far exceeds ours as their situations are exalted above ours, we humbly, respectfully, and fervently entreat and beseech your disapprobation of the plan of colonization now offered by The American Society for Colonizing the Free People of Color of the United States.

There Is No Manhood Future in the United States for the Negro (1895)*

Henry M. Turner

Henry M. Turner, Bishop of the African Methodist Episcopal Church, served in the Reconstruction legislature in Georgia. After the overthrow of Reconstruction and the abandonment of the effort to guarantee equal rights for the Negro in America, Turner helped to revive the separatist doctrines that flourished before the Civil War. He was the most prominent advocate of African emigration in the closing years of the nineteenth century.

In this address before an organization devoted to emigration and missionary activities in Africa, Bishop Turner presented an argument that the emigration of American Negroes to Africa would benefit both areas.

It would be a waste of time to expend much labor, the few moments I have to devote to this subject, upon the present status of the Negroid race in the United States. It is too well known already. However, I believe that the Negro was brought to this country in the providence of God to a heaven-permitted if not a divine-sanctioned manual laboring school, that he might have direct contact with the mightiest race that ever trod the face of the globe.

The heathen Africans, to my certain knowledge, I care not what others may say, eagerly yearn for that civilization which they believe will elevate them and make them potential for good. The African was not sent and brought to this country by chance, or by the avarice of the White man, single and alone. The White slave-purchaser went to the shores of that continent and brought our ancestors from their African masters. The bulk who were brought to this country were the children of parents who had been in slavery a thousand years. Yet hereditary slavery is not universal among the African slaveholders. So that the argument often advanced, that the White man went to Africa and stole us, is not true. They bought us out of a slavery that still exists over a large portion of that continent. For there are millions and millions of slaves in

---

* Henry M. Turner, "The American Negro and the Fatherland," in J.W.E. Bowen, ed., *Addresses and Proceedings of the Congress on Africa* (Atlanta, Georgia: Gammon Theological Seminary, 1896), pp. 195–198.

Africa today. Thus the superior African sent us, and the White man brought us, and we remained in slavery as long as it was necessary to learn that a God, who is a spirit, made the world and controls it, and that that Supreme Being could be sought and found by the exercise of faith in His only begotten Son. Slavery then went down, and the Colored man was thrown upon his own responsibility, and here he is today, in the providence of God, cultivating self-reliance and imbibing a knowledge of civil law in contradistinction to the dictum of one man, which was the law of the Black man until slavery was overthrown. I believe that the Negroid race has been free long enough now to begin to think for himself and plan for better conditions than he can lay claim to in this country or ever will. *There is no manhood future in the United States for the Negro.* He may eke out an existence for generations to come, but he can never be a *man*—full, symmetrical and undwarfed. Upon this point I know thousands who make pretensions to scholarship, White and Colored, will differ and may charge me with folly, while I in turn pity their ignorance of history and political and civil sociology. We beg here to itemize and give a cursory glance at a few facts calculated to convince any man who is not biased or lamentably ignorant. Let us note a few of them.

I

There is a great chasm between the White and Black, not only in this country, but in the West India Islands, South America, and as much as has been said to the contrary, I have seen inklings of it in Ireland, in England, in France, in Germany, and even away down in southern Spain in sight of Morocco in Africa. We will not however deal with foreign nations, but let us note a few facts connected with the United States.

I repeat that a great chasm exists between the two race varieties in this country. The White people, neither North nor South, will have social contact as a mass between themselves and any portion of the Negroid race. Although they may be as white in appearance as themselves, yet a drop of African blood imparts a taint, and the talk about two races remaining in the same country with mutual interest and responsibility in its institutions and progress, with no social contact, is the jargon of folly, and no man who has read the history of nations and the development of countries, and the agencies which have culminated in the homogeneity of racial variations, will proclaim such a doctrine. Senator Morgan of Alabama tells the truth when he says that the Negro has nothing to expect without social equality with the Whites, and that the Whites will never grant it.

This question must be examined and opinions reached in the light of history and sociological philosophy, and not be a mere think-so on the part of men devoid of learning. When I use the term "learning," I do not refer to men who have graduated from some college and have a smattering knowledge of Greek, Latin, mathematics and a few school books, and have done nothing since but read the trashy articles of newspapers. That is not scholarship. Scholarship consists in wading through dusty volumes for forty and fifty years. That class of men would not dare to predict symmetrical manhood for the Negroid race in this or any other country, without social equality. The Colored man who will stand up and in one breath say that the Negroid race does not want social equality, and in the next predict a great future in the face of all the proscription of which the Colored man is the victim, is either an ignoramus, or is an advocate of the perpetual servility and degradation of his race variety. I know, as Senator Morgan says, and as every White man in the land will say, that the Whites will not grant social equality to the Negroid race, nor am I certain that God wants them to do it. And as such, I believe that two or three millions of us should return to the land of our ancestors, and establish our own nation, civilization, laws, customs, style of manufacture, and not only give the world, like other race varieties, the benefit of our individuality, but build up social conditions peculiarly our own, and cease to be grumblers, chronic complainers and a menace to the White man's country, or the country he claims and is bound to dominate.

The civil status of the Negro is simply what the White man grants of his own free will and accord. The Black man can demand nothing. He is deposed from the jury and tried, convicted and sentenced by men who do not claim to be his peers. On the railroads, where the Colored race is found in the largest numbers, he is the victim of proscription, and he must ride in the Jim Crow car or walk. The Supreme Court of the United States decided, October 15, 1882, that the Colored man had no civil rights under the general government, and the several states, from then until now, have been enacting laws which limit, curtail and deprive him of his civil rights, immunities and privileges, until he is now being disfranchised, and where it will end no one can divine.

They told me in the Geographical Institute in Paris, France, that according to their calculation there are less than 400,000,000 of Africans and their descendants on the globe, so that we are not lacking in numbers to form a nationality of our own.

II

The environments of the Negroid race variety in this country tend to the inferiority of them, even if the argument can be established that we are equals with the White man in the aggregate, notwithstanding the same opportunities may be enjoyed in the schools. Let us note a few facts.

The discriminating laws, all will concede, are degrading to those against whom they operate, and the degrader will be degraded also. "For all acts are reactionary, and will return in curses upon those who curse," said Stephen A. Douglas, the great competitor of President Lincoln. Neither does it require a philosopher to inform you that degradation begets degradation. Any people oppressed, proscribed, belied, slandered, burned, flayed and lynched will not only become cowardly and servile, but will transmit that same servility to their posterity, and continue to do so *ad infinitum,* and as such will never make a bold and courageous people. The condition of the Negro in the United States is so repugnant to the instincts of respected manhood that thousands, yea hundreds of thousands, of miscegenated will pass for White, and snub the people with whom they are identified at every opportunity, thus destroying themselves, or at least *unracing* themselves. They do not want to be Black because of its ignoble condition, and they cannot be White, thus they become monstrosities. Thousands of young men who are even educated by White teachers never have any respect for people of their own color and spend their days as devotees of White gods. Hundreds, if not thousands, of the terms employed by the White race in the English language are also degrading to the Black man. Everything that is satanic, corrupt, base and infamous is denominated *black,* and all that constitutes virtue, purity, innocence, religion, and that which is divine and heavenly, is represented as *white.* Our Sabbath-school children, by the time they reach proper consciousness, are taught to sing the laudation of white and to the contempt of black. Can any one with an ounce of common sense expect that these children, when they reach maturity, will ever have any respect for their black or colored faces, or the faces of their associates? But without multiplying words, the terms used in our religious experience, and the hymns we sing in many instances, are degrading, and will be as long as the Black man is surrounded by the idea that *white* represents God and *black* represents the devil. The Negro should, therefore, build up a nation of his own, and create a language in keeping with his color, as the Whites have done. Nor will he ever respect himself until he does it.

III

In this country the Colored man, with a few honorable exceptions, folds his arms and waits for the White man to propose, project, erect, invent, discover, combine, plan and execute everything connected with civilization, including machinery, finance, and indeed everything. This, in the nature of things, dwarfs the Colored man and allows his great faculties to slumber from the cradle to the grave. Yet he possesses mechanical and inventive genius, I believe, equal to any race on earth. Much has been said about the natural inability of the Colored race to engage in the professions of skilled labor. Yet before the war, right here in this southland, he erected and completed all of the fine edifices in which the lords of the land luxuriated. It is idle talk to speak of a Colored man not being a success in skilled labor or the fine arts. What the Black man needs is a country and surroundings in harmony with his color and with respect for his manhood. Upon this point I would delight to dwell longer if I had time. Thousands of white people in this country are ever and anon advising the colored people to keep out of politics, but they do not advise themselves. If the Negro is a man in keeping with other men, why should he be less concerned about politics than any one else? . . . If the Negro is to be a man, full and complete, he must take part in everything that belongs to manhood. If he omits a single duty, responsibility or privilege, to that extent he is limited and incomplete.

. . . I conclude by saying the argument that it would be impossible to transport the colored people of the United States back to Africa is an advertisement of folly. Two hundred millions of dollars would rid this country of the last member of the Negroid race, if such a thing was desirable, and 250 millions would give every man, woman and child excellent fare, and the general government could furnish that amount and never miss it, and that would only be the pitiful sum of a million dollars a year for the time we labored for nothing, and for which somebody or some power is responsible. The emigrant agents at New York, Boston, Philadelphia, St. John, New Brunswick, and Halifax, Nova Scotia, with whom I have talked, established beyond contradiction, that over a million, and from that to 1.2 million persons, come to this country every year, and yet there is no public stir about it. But in the case of African emigration, two or three millions only of self-reliant men and women would be necessary to establish the conditions we are advocating in Africa.

Chapter Three

Black Radicalism in the Early Twentieth Century

At the dawn of the twentieth century three-quarters of the Black population of the United States lived in rural areas, nine-tenths of them in the southern states where they were directly subject to extreme political oppression and physical terrorism. But the Great Migration that would make three-quarters of them city dwellers and bring a majority to the North by the 1960's had already begun. The sudden, disorienting shift of the center of Negro life to the teeming northern slums and the enormous social and economic pressures placed on them there, provided fertile ground for the seeds of radical discontent.

During the First World War, hundreds of thousands of Negro youths fought "to make the world safe for democracy" and in the process sampled a more open and liberal atmosphere in Europe. Many returned home determined to achieve at home the principles they had fought for abroad, only to meet with intensified racial oppression. White mobs, resisting the increasing flood of Negro migrants to the North, burned, looted and murdered in the ghetto areas of numerous cities during the summer of 1919. The Ku Klux Klan achieved its greatest influence by the mid-twenties and in the same period the federal government completed its capitulation to racism by enacting immigration

restrictions frankly based on theories of Nordic superiority. Under those intellectual and moral pressures, the Negro community, which had been sunk
in quiescent apathy twenty years earlier, seethed with anger and ideological
conflict.

The changed mood of the Black people evidenced itself during the racial
violence in 1919.* In many areas Negroes retaliated vigorously against White
agressors and their efforts were applauded by the traditionally cautious Negro
press. "Any Negro," wrote a Virginia editor,

> who says that he is satisfied to be let alone with his broken political
> power, his miserable Jim Crow restrictions, his un-American segregation,
> his . . . emasculated democracy, and his blood curdling inquisition of
> lynching, simply lies. He lies basely. He knows himself he lies, and the White
> man knows he lies. He does not fool anybody. He disgusts his friends, and
> earns only the contempt of those whose favor he seeks to win. He assumes
> this contemptible attitude not because he is feeble minded, however, but be-
> cause he has a white liver. He is an arrant coward and a traitor besides.†

"When the Negro," said a Pittsburg journal,

> went to France and there laid down his life along with all other Americans
> for the salvation of France and the establishment of Democracy à la
> Wilson, he learned that any man who could, by his blood, purchase lib-
> erty for France and England, could, by the shedding of enough of the
> same blood, purchase liberty and freedom for himself in his own
> country.**

In Houston, Texas, a Negro paper stated that

> The man who can see no reason for the colored Americans unrest and
> dissatisfaction is either a mental misfit or totally unacquainted with
> human psychology . . . When called upon to defend his country's honor
> and integrity and to save civilization from the clutches of the cruel and
> heartless Huns of Europe, the Black American [went] forth to battle the
> mighty goliath of autocracy, militarism and Kultur. Having performed a
> "brown-skin" job "over there" he now expects Unce Sam to clean up his
> own premises and since the Black man fought to make the world safe for
> Democracy, he now demands that America be made and maintained safe
> for Black Americans.††

---

* More detailed consideration of these and other disturbances can be found
in *Urban Racial Violence in the Twentieth Century* by Joseph Boskin, another
Insight Series book.

† *Newport News Star* (October 3, 1919).

** *Pittsburg Courier* (October 25, 1919).

†† *Houston Informer* (October 11, 1919).

By the mid-twenties a variety of protest movements contended for the attention of the confused and angry Black masses. Twenty years earlier, Booker T. Washington, preaching accommodation to existing prejudices and the gradual preparation of the Negro for equality through moral improvement and economic self-help, had enjoyed an unchallenged position as the spokesman for his race.† By the 1920's, the remnants of Washington's Tuskegee machine was defending its conservative position against attacks from all sides.** The NAACP, pledged to press the fight against all forms of discrimination by legal means and was itself attacked by a Marxist-oriented group, headed by A. Philip Randolph, that advocated proletarian revolution. Marcus Garvey's Universal Negro Improvement Association advanced a radical Black Nationalist program that envisaged the liberation and unification of Africa and the repatriation of the American Negro population. "The Negro schools of thought," wrote Randolph, "are torn with dissension, giving birth to many insurgent factions."†† The documents in this chapter deal primarily with those ideological conflicts, during which the nineteenth-century revolutionary and separatist traditions were revived and vastly expanded.

The Conservation of Races (1897)*

W. E. B. Du Bois

One of the first and the most effective of the opponents of Booker T. Washington's accommodationist leadership, Du Bois began in this essay to develop the strong racial consciousness that would lead him in increasingly radical directions. In 1903 he published his influential *The Souls of Black Folk* and in 1905 founded, with the radical newspaperman James Monroe Trotter and others, the Niagra Movement. The NAACP grew out of that organization

---

† Francis L. Broderick and August Meier, eds., *Negro Protest Thought*, in *the Twentieth Century* (Indianapolis: Bobbs-Merrill, 1965), pp. 177–181.

** Washington believed that the Negro could advance himself by being an efficient worker and by educating himself. Therefore, Tuskegee Institute, of which Washington was president from 1881–1915, taught a number of trades and professions as well as academic subjects. Its enrollment in 1968 was 2,612.

†† Quoted in August Meier and Elliot M. Rudwick, *From Plantation to Ghetto* (New York: Hill and Wang, 1966), p. 221.

* W. E. B. Du Bois, "The Conservation of Races," *The American Negro Academy, Occasional Papers*, No. II (Washington, D.C.: 1897).

and Du Bois became and remained for many years the editor of its magazine, *The Crisis*, although his own ideas, increasingly influenced by Pan-African and Marxist thought, soon diverged from those of the main body of the Association.

The American Negro has always felt an intense personal interest in discussions as to the origins and destinies of races: primarily because back of most discussions of race with which he is familiar, have lurked certain assumptions as to his natural abilities, as to his political, intellectual and moral status, which he felt were wrong. He has, consequently, been led to deprecate and minimize race distinction, to believe intensely that out of one blood God created all nations, and to speak of human brotherhood as though it were the possibility of an already dawning tomorrow.

Nevertheless, in our calmer moments we must acknowledge that human beings are divided into races; that in this country the two most extreme types of the world's races have met, and the resulting problem as to the future relations of these types is not only of intense and living interest to us, but forms an epoch in the history of mankind.

It is necessary, therefore, in planning our movements, in guiding our future development, that at times we rise above the pressing, but smaller questions of separate schools and cars, wage-discrimination and lynch law, to survey the whole question of race in human philosophy and to lay, on a basis of broad knowledge and careful insight, those large lines of policy and higher ideals which may form our guiding lines and boundaries in the practical difficulties of every day. For it is certain that all human striving, no matter how intense and earnest, which is against the constitution of the world, is vain. The question, then, which we must seriously consider is this: What is the real meaning of *race;* what has, in the past, been the law of development; and what lessons has the past history of race development to teach the rising Negro people?

When we thus come to inquire into the essential difference of races we find it hard to come at once to any definite conclusion. Many criteria of race differences have in the past been proposed, as color, hair, cranial measurements and language. And manifestly, in each of these respects, human beings differ widely. They vary in color, for instance, from the marble-like pallor of the Scandinavian to the rich, dark brown of the Zulu, passing by the creamy Slav, the yellow Chinese, the light-brown Sicilian and the brown Egyptian. Men vary, too, in the texture of hair from the obstinately straight hair of the Chinese to the obstinately tufted and frizzled hair of the Bushman. In measurement of heads, again, men vary; from the broad-headed Tartar to the medium-headed European and the narrowheaded Hottentot; or again in language, from the highly inflected Roman tongue to the monosyllabic Chinese. All these physical characteristics are patent enough, and if they agreed with each other it would be very easy to classify mankind. Unfortunately for scientists, however, these criteria of race are most exasperatingly intermingled. Color does not agree with texture of hair, for many of the dark races have straight hair; nor does color agree with the breadth of the head, for the yellow Tartar has a broader head than the German; nor again, has the science of language as yet succeeded in clearing up the relative authority of these various and contradictory criteria. The final word of science, so far, is that we have at least two, perhaps three, great families of human beings—the Whites and Negroes, possibly the yellow race. The other races have arisen from the intermingling of the blood of these two. This broad division of the world's races which men like Huxley and Raetzel have introduced as more nearly true than the old five-race scheme of Blumenbach,* is nothing more than an acknowledgment that, so far as purely physical characteristics are concerned, the differences between men do not explain all the differences of their history. It declares, as Darwin himself said, that great as is the physical unlikeness of the various races of men their likenesses are greater, and upon this rests the whole scientific doctrine of human brotherhood.

Although the wonderful developments of human history teach that the grosser physical differences of color, hair and bone go but a short way toward explaining the different roles which groups of men have played in human progress, yet there are differences — subtle, delicate and elusive, though they may be—which have silently but definitely separated men into groups. While these subtle forces have generally followed the natural cleavage of common

---

* Friedrich Raetzel (1844–1904), a German philosopher, was best known for his theory that cultures grow through diffusion (borrowing). Thomas Henry Haxley (1825–1895) was an English biologist and philosopher, a supporter of Darwinian evolutionary theory.

blood, descent and physical peculiarities, they have at other times swept across and ignored these. At all times, however, they have divided human beings into races, which while they perhaps transcend scientific definition, nevertheless, are clearly defined to the eye of the historian and sociologist.

If this be true, then the history of the world is the history, not of individuals, but of groups, not of nations, but of races, and he who ignores or seeks to override the race idea in human history ignores and overrides the central thought of all history. What, then, is a race? It is a vast family of human beings, generally of common blood and language, always of common history, traditions and impulses, who are both voluntarily and involuntarily striving together for the accomplishment of certain more or less vividly conceived ideals of life.

Turning to real history, there can be no doubt, first, as to the widespread, nay, universal, prevalence of the race ideas, the race spirit, the race ideal, and as to its efficiency as the vastest and most ingenious invention for human progress. We, who have been reared and trained under the individualistic philosophy of the Declaration of Independence and the laisser-faire philosophy of Adam Smith, are loath to see and loath to acknowledge this patent fact of human history. We see the Pharaohs, Caesars, Toussaints and Napoleons of history and forget the vast races of which they were but epitomized expressions. We are apt to think in our American impatience, that while it may have been true in the past that closed race groups make history, that here in conglomerate America *nous avons changé tout cela*—we have changed all that—and have no need of this ancient instrument of progress. This assumption of which the Negro people are especially fond, can not be established by a careful consideration of history.

We find upon the world's stage today eight distinctly differentiated races, in the sense in which history tells us the word must be used. They are, the Slavs of eastern Europe, the Teutons of middle Europe, the English of Great Britain and America, the Romance nations of Southern and Western Europe, the Negroes of Africa and America, the Hindus of Central Asia and the Mongolians of Eastern Asia. There are, of course, other minor race groups, as the American Indians, the Eskimo and the South Sea Islanders; these larger races, too, are far from homogeneous; the Slav includes the

Czech, the Magyar, the Pole and the Russian; the Teuton includes the German, the Scandinavian and the Dutch; the English include the Scotch, the Irish and the conglomerate American. Under Romance nations the widely differing Frenchman, Italian, Sicilian and Spaniard are comprehended. The term "Negro" is perhaps, the most indefinite of all, combining the Mulattoes and Zamboes of America and the Egyptians, Bantus and Bushmen of Africa. Among the Hindus are traces of widely differing nations, while the great Chinese, Tartar, Korean and Japanese families fall under the one designation—Mongolian.

The question now is: What is the real distinction between these nations? Is it the physical differences of blood, color and cranial measurements? Certainly we must all acknowledge that physical differences play a great part, and that, with wide exceptions and qualifications, these eight great races of today follow the cleavage of physical race distinctions; the English and Teuton represent the White variety of mandkind; the Mongolian, the Yellow; the Negroes, the Black. Between these are many crosses and mixtures where Mongolian and Teuton have blended into the Slav, and other mixtures have produced the Romance nations and the Semites. But while race differences have followed mainly physical race lines, yet no mere physical distinctions would really define or explain the deeper differences—the cohesiveness and continuity of these groups. The deeper differences are spiritual, psychical—differences undoubtedly based on the physical, but infinitely transcending them. The forces that bind together the Teuton nations are, then, first, their race identity and common blood; secondly, and more important, a common history, common laws and religion, similar habits of thought and a conscious striving together for certain ideals of life. The whole process which has brought about these race differentiations has been a growth, and the great characteristic of this growth has been the differentiation of spiritual and mental differences between great races of mankind and the integration of physical differences.

The age of nomadic tribes of closely related individuals represents the maximum of physical differences. They were practically vast families, and there were as many groups as families. As the families came together to form cities the physical differences lessened, purity of blood was replaced by the requirement of domicile, and all who lived within the city bounds became gradually to be regarded as members of the group; *i.e.*, there was a slight and slow breaking down of physical barriers. This, however, was accompanied by an increase of the spiritual and social differences between cities. This city became husbandmen, this, merchants, another warriors, and so on. The *ideals of life* for which the different cities struggled were different. When at last cities began to coalesce into nations there was another breaking down of barriers which separated groups of men. The larger and broader differences of color, hair and physical proportions were not by any means ignored, but myriads of minor differences disappeared, and the sociological and historical races of men began to approximate the present division of races as indicated by physical researches. At the same time the spiritual and physical differences of race groups which constituted the nations became deep and decisive. The English nation stood for constitutional liberty and commercial freedom; the German nation for science and philosophy; the Romance nations stood for literature and art, and the other race groups are striving, each in its own way, to develop for civilization its particular message, its particular ideal, which shall help to guide the world nearer and nearer that perfection of human life for which we all long, that "one far-off Divine event."

This has been the function of race differences up to the present time. What shall be its function in the future? Manifestly some of the great races of today—particularly the Negro race—have not as yet given to civilization the full spiritual message which they are capable of giving. I will not say that the Negro race has as yet given no message to the world, for it is still a mooted question among scientists as to just how far Egyptian civilization was Negro in its origin; if it was not wholly Negro, it was certainly very closely allied. Be that as it may, however the fact still remains that the full, complete Negro message of the whole Negro race has not as yet been given to the world: that the messages and ideal of the Yellow race have not been completed, and that the striving of the mighty Slavs has but begun. The question is, then: How shall this message be delivered; how shall these various ideals be realized? The answer is plain: by the development of these race groups, not as individuals, but as races. For the development of Japanese genius, Japanese literature and art, Japanese spirit, only Japanese, bound and welded together, Japanese inspired by one vast ideal, can work out in its fullness the wonderful message which Japan has for the nations of the earth. For the development of Negro genius, of Negro literature and art, of Negro spirit, only Negroes bound and welded together, Negroes inspired by one vast ideal, can work out in its fullness the great message we have for humanity. We cannot reverse history; we are subject to the same natural laws as other races, and if the Negro is ever to be a factor in the world's history—if among the gaily colored banners that deck the broad ramparts of civilization is to hang one uncompromising black—then it must be placed there by Black hands, fashioned by Black heads and hallowed by the travail of 200,000,000 Black hearts beating in one glad song of jubilee.

For this reason, the advance guard of the Negro people—the 8 million people of Negro blood in the United States of America— must soon come to realize that if they are to take their just place in the van of Pan-Negroism, then their destiny is *not* absorption by the White Americans. That if in America it is to be proven for the first time in the modern world that not only Negroes are capable of evolving individual men like Toussaint, the saviour, but are a nation stored with wonderful possibilities of culture, then their destiny is not a servile imitation of Anglo-Saxon culture, but a stalwart originality which shall unswervingly follow Negro ideals.

It may, however, be objected here that the situation of our race in America renders this attitude impossible; that our sole hope of salvation lies in our being able to lose our race identity in the com-mingled blood of the nation; and that any other course would merely increase the friction of races which we call race prejudice, and against which we have so long and so earnestly fought.

Here, then is the dilemma, and it is a puzzling one, I admit. No Negro who has given earnest thought to the situation of his people in America has failed, at some time in life, to find himself at these crossroads; has failed to ask himself at some time: What, after all, am I? Am I an American or am I a Negro? Can I be both? Or is it my duty to cease to be a Negro as soon as possible and be an American? If I strive as a Negro, am I not perpetuating the very cleft that threatens and separates Black and White America? Is not my only possible practical aim the subduction of all that is Negro in me to the American? Does my Black blood place upon me any more obligation to assert my nationality than German, or Irish or Italian blood would?

It is such incessant self-questioning and the hesitation that arises from it, that is making the present period a time of vacillation and contradiction for the American Negro; combined race action is stiffed, race responsibility is shirked, race enterprises languish, and the best blood, the best talent, the best energy of the Negro people cannot be marshaled to do the bidding of the race. They stand back to make room for every rascal and demagogue who chooses to cloak his selfish deviltry under the veil of race pride.

Is this right? Is it rational? Is it good policy? Have we in America a distinct mission as a race—a distinct sphere of action and an opportunity for race development, or is self-obliteration the highest end to which Negro blood dare aspire?

If we carefully consider what race prejudice really is, we find it, historically, to be nothing but the friction between different groups of people; it is the difference in air, in feeling, in ideals of two different races; if, now, this difference exists touching territory, laws, language, or even religion, it is manifest that these people cannot live in the same territory without fatal collision; but if, on the other hand, there is substantial agreement in laws, language and religion; if there is a satisfactory adjustment of economic life, then there is no reason why, in the same country and on the same street, two or three great national ideals might not thrive and develop, that men of different races might not strive together for their race ideals as well, perhaps even better, than in isolation. Here, it seems to me, is the reading of the riddle that puzzles so many of us. We are Americans, not only by birth and by citizenship, but by our political ideals, our language, our religion. Farther than that, our Americanism does not go. At that point, we are Negroes, members of a vast historic race that from the very dawn of creation has slept, but half awakening, in the dark forests of its African fatherland. We are the first fruits of this new nation, the harbinger of that Black tomorrow which is yet destined to soften the whiteness of the Teutonic today. We are that people whose subtle sense of song has given America its only American music, its only American fairy tales, its only touch of pathos and humor amid its mad money-getting plutocracy. As such, it is our duty to conserve our physical powers, our intellectual endowments, our spiritual ideals; as a race we must strive by race organization, by race solidarity, by race unity to the realization of that broader humanity which freely recognizes differences in men, but sternly deprecates inequality in their opportunities of development.

For the accomplishment of these ends we need race organizations: Negro colleges, Negro newspapers, Negro business organizations, a Negro school of literature and art, and an intellectual clearinghouse, for all these products of the Negro mind, which we may call a Negro Academy. Not only is all this necessary for positive advance, it is absolutely imperative for negative defense. Let us not deceive ourselves at our situation in this country. Weighted with a heritage of moral iniquity from our past history, hard pressed in the economic world by foreign immigrants and native prejudice, hated here, despised there and pitied everywhere; our one haven of refuge is ourselves, and but one means of advance, our own belief in our great destiny, our own implicit trust in our ability and worth. There is no power under God's high heaven than can stop the advance of eight thousand thousand honest, earnest, inspired and united people. But—and here is the rub—they *must* be honest, fearlessly criticising their own faults, zealously correcting them; they must be *earnest*. No people that laughs at itself, and ridicules itself, and wishes to God it was anything but itself ever wrote its name in history; it *must* be inspired with the divine faith of our Black mothers, that out of the Black mothers, that out of the blood and dust of battle will march a victorious host, a mighty nation, a peculiar people, to speak to the nations of earth a Divine truth that shall make them free. And such a people must be united; not merely united for the organized theft of political spoils, not united to disgrace religion with whoremongers and ward heelers; not united merely to protest and pass resolutions, but united to stop the ravages of consumption among the Negro people, united to keep Black boys from loafing, gambling, and crime; united to guard the purity of Black women and to reduce that vast army of Black prostitutes that is today marching to hell; and united in serious organizations, to determine by careful conference and thoughtful interchange of opinion the broad lines of policy and action for the American Negro.

This, is the reason for being which the American Negro Academy has. It aims at once to be the epitome and expression of the intellect of the Black blooded people of America, the exponent of the race ideals of one of the world's greatest races. As such, the Academy must, if successful, be (a) representative in character; (b) impartial in conduct; (c) firm in leadership.

It must be representative in character; not in that it represents all interests or factions, but in that it seeks to comprise something of the *best* thought, the most unselfish striving and the highest ideals. There are scattered in forgotten nooks and corners throughout the land, Negroes of some considerable training, of high minds, and high motives, who are unknown to their fellows, who exert far too little influence. These the Negro Academy should strive to bring into touch with each other and to give them a common mouthpiece.

The Academy should be impartial in conduct; while it aims to exalt the people it should aim to do so by truth—not by lies, by honesty—not by flattery. It should continually impress the fact upon the Negro people that they must not expect to have things done for them—they *must do for themselves:* that they have on their hands a vast work of self-reformation to do, and that a little less complaint and whining, and a little more dogged work and manly striving would do us more credit and benefit than a thousand Force or Civil Rights bills.

Finally, the American Negro Academy must point out a practical path of advance to the Negro people; there lie before every Negro today hundreds of questions of policy and right which must be settled and which each one settles now, not in accordance with any rule, but by impulse or individual preference; for instance: What should be the attitude of Negroes toward the educational qualification for voters? What should be our attitude toward separate schools? How should we meet discrimination on railways and in hotels? Such questions need not so much specific answers for each part as a general expression of policy, and nobody should be better fitted to announce such a policy than a representative honest Negro Academy.

All this, however, must come in time after careful organization and long conference. The immediate work before us should be practical and have direct bearing upon the situation of the Negro. The historical work of collecting the laws of the United States and of the various States of the Union with regard to the Negro is a work of such magnitude and importance that no body but one like this could think of undertaking it. If we could accomplish that one task we would justify our existence.

In the field of sociology an appalling work lies before us. First, we must unflinchingly and bravely face the truth, not with apologies, but with solemn earnestness. The Negro Academy ought to sound a note of warning that would echo in every Black cabin in the land: *Unless we conquer our present vices they will conquer us;* we are diseased, we are developing criminal tendencies, and an alarmingly large percentage of our men and women are sexually impure. The Negro Academy should stand and proclaim this over the housetops, crying with Garrison: *I will not equivocate, I will not retreat a single inch, and I will be heard.* The Academy should seek to gather about it the talented, unselfish men, the pure and noble-minded women, to fight an army of devils that disgraces our manhood and our womanhood. There does not stand today upon God's earth a race more capable in muscle, in intellect, in morals, than the American Negro, if he will bend his engeries in the right direction; if he will

> Burst his birth's invidious bar
> And grasp the skirts of happy chance,
> And breast the blows of circumstance;
> And grapple with his evil star.

In science and morals, I have indicated two fields of work for the Academy. Finally, in practical policy, I wish to suggest the following *Academy Creed*:

1) We believe that the Negro people, as a race, have a contribution to make to civilization and humanity, which no other race can make.

2) We believe it the duty of the Americans of Negro descent, as a body, to maintain their race identity until this mission of the Negro people is accomplished, and the ideal of human brotherhood has become a practical possibility.

3) We believe that, unless modern civilization is a failure, it is entirely feasible and practicable for two races in such essential political, economic, and religious harmony as the White and Colored people of America, to develop side by side in peace and mutual happiness, the peculiar contribution which each has to make to the culture of

their common country.

4) As a means to this end, we advocate, not such social equality between these races as would disregard human likes and dislikes, but such a social equilibrium as would, throughout all the complicated relations of life, give due and just consideration to culture, ability, and moral worth, whether they be found under white or black skins.

5) We believe that the first and greatest step toward the settlement of the present friction between the races—commonly called the Negro Problem—lies in the correction of the immorality, crime and laziness among the Negroes themselves, which still remains as a heritage from slavery. We believe that only earnest and long continued efforts on our own part can cure these social ills.

6) We believe that the second great step toward a better adjustment of the relations between the races, should be a more impartial selection of ability in the economic and intellectual world, and a greater respect for personal liberty and worth, regardless of race. We believe that only earnest efforts on the part of the White people of this country will bring much needed reform in these matters.

7) On the basis of the foregoing declaration, and firmly believing in our high destiny, we, as American Negroes, are firmly resolved to strive in every honorable way for the realizations of the best and highest aims, for the development of strong manhood and pure womanhood, and for the rearing of a race ideal in America and Africa, to the glory of God and the uplifting of the Negro people.

The Nationalism of the New Negro (1920)*

Oswald Z. Parris

Stimulated by the cultural impact of the First World War and the mass movement of the Negro population from the rural South to the urban ghettoes of the North, nationalist sentiments began to spread rapidly in the early 1920's. The following document, taken from a book by Oswald Z. Parris, principal of the Virginia School of Music, reflects those influences.

If it be true that the causes which tend to Negro dissension can be remedied, then let us, in all honesty and goodwill, review a few facts for our common good. With such examples as the heroic Irish, the unfortunate Indians, and the overawed Egyptians before us, it really seems as if the Negro—especially the American Negro, the most advanced of the race—is less concerned about his cause or condition than any other race on the face of the earth, when this is not the case.

Unfortunately (yet, maybe fortunately) for us, we were stolen from our native shores, and taken to the West Indies and this country by no consent of our own. After years of a condition which could not last indefinitely, we were clothed with a semblance of freedom. Then came the time when it suited the White man to play off the southern Negro against the northern Negro. Turning this lesson to good account, we find the southern Negro hating the northern Negro, and the northern Negro hating the western Negro; and the American Negro hating the West Indian Negro, and vice versa.

Another factor contributing to Negro dissension, is the custom of Negroes of the same section holding aloof from others of the race on account of shade—the mulatto holding himself superior to the high Brown, who, in turn, holds himself superior to the fast Black. It is deplorable, the harm this fatuity works to the race. What can a race amount to, with such a faction as those who would deny intercourse to any but the "light-colored?" We do not kick at the presence of the rational class of "light-colored" in the race. But

---

* Oswald Z. Parris, *The Nationalism of the New Negro* (Newport News, Va.: Oswald Z. Parris Co., 1920), pp. 9–17.

from the beginning, the other class has been an evil. We are proud to know that there is a large number of Negroes of mixed blood, who are as African as the blackest. But to the others who practice the ill-feeling complained of above, I make no apologies. These poor unfortunates do not want to belong to the Negro race; and the White race certainly does not want them. But take courage, brother. In Africa there are tribes so light in complexion, that ethnologists are puzzled over their existence. And these tribes know no other land but Africa.

Then, too, one member of the race hates to see another progress. Jealousy and hatred are the instruments with which we murder each other. Too many of us want to be leaders; too few, followers.

Again, we have been taught from infancy that the White man is our superior. In our homes, the first pictures we see on the walls, are those of White men and women; the toys we first play with, are toys which keep the picture of the White man before us all the time —dolls, images, etc. Cannot the parents do something to correct this? In school, we learn of the White man's prowess, his heroes and all. We never know of a L'Ouverture, or a Cetewayo.*

Another factor to be considered is the religious training our race has been receiving. In the early days of our freedom, a large number of men, being full of religious fervor, and seeing the need for spiritual leadership in the race, undertook to supply that want. These men believed they were called to the divine office regardless of their fitness. They used the term "called to preach" to such an extent, that today, it has become a byword (by way of apology) among those who, without any preparation what ever, attempt to expound the Holy Scriptures. These men of old did the best they could. They were equal to their congregations. But in these days, when the young Negro is excelling in higher education, the men of the old school find themselves far behind their congregations. This is the cause of the many empty pews today.

The modern preacher must keep up with the congregation. When you consider how English has changed since the Elizabethan days— one being hardly able now to read or understand a script of that

---

* Cetewayo (d. 1884), was recognized by the British as king of the Zulus in 1872, but rebelled in 1878 against British rule and destroyed a British regiment at Isandhlwana in 1879. He was captured in the same year, taken to England three years later, and never regained his authority.

period—how inconceivable it is that men without even a correct ideal of present day English, should be able to go back into past English literature, and then into the Latin, Greek, and Hebrew language for correct interpretation of the Writ. Even men of learning must prepare their sermons with the aid of commentaries and concordances.

While I have every respect for the clergy of whatever state, I cannot agree with those who preach that the Negro must passively pray and pray. I believe in prayer with work. I refuse to accept the teaching that God intended the Negro to be always a servant of slaves. But I assure you, my readers, that if we do nothing to bring about a better condition for our posterity, we shall have to give God an account for it.

Last, but not least, among some of the causes contributory to Negro dissension, is the fact that we lack real leaders. Whenever a leader arises among us, the White man hastens to buy him off with some small office, or special favor, thereby effectively closing his mouth and conscience, too. Then when a real leader comes on the scene, these pseudo-leaders, in obedience to their White masters, poison the mind of the masses against him.

You ask me what have these facts to do with the New Negro. Well, the answer is: Let us, without prejudice, examine these facts, and see if they be true of any other race; and if not, then let us conscientiously take steps to remove the evil, so that we might stand together in this momentous period, and make good our destinies. We might sometimes wonder why did God permit us to be brought to this country to suffer as we do. Perhaps, herein was a blessing in disguise; for today the American Negro is the most advanced of his race and well fitted, though training and experience, to lead in the cause for national recognition.

From the foregoing, it is obvious that the Negro race lacks the unity and race-consciousness that go to make up a nation. Now and then, in resentment of some wrong, real or imaginary, on the part of the White man in America, we hear such slogans as "get together" or "organize." But soon the fever cools off, and we sink back into our condition of complacency. Once in a while, some of the leaders come out with the advice, whether to become all democrats, or all republicans, as a means of whipping the government into line to grant us our petitions. Then another will suggest that

we stay away from the polls altogether. Sometimes, we get so far
as to organize committees for the purpose of presenting grievances
before some mayor, or even the President. And we do succeed in
getting a hearing—and that is all. Some refer to segregation, and
suggest, as the White people have segregated us, we ought to further
segregate ourselves by refusing to do businss with them, thereby
building up our own enterprises and spiting the White people. I do
not know if this method of protesting will help any. It is not feasible
to the Negro race to carry on business enterprises wholly and apart
from the other race. False remedies!

The whole trouble is this, that 13 million Negroes are trying
to force on 102 million White people to grant us privileges and
rights equal to their own, when there is a constitutional antipathy
on the part of the greater race toward the lesser. We are simply
forcing ourselves on the White man because, we say, he brought us
here. But we forget that hundreds of years ago, the White man
came to this country; and, forcing the natives back, established for
himself a home, a country, enduring hardships and privations to
accomplish this. This is his country, if we allow it. Do we suppose
that he is now going to lightly give an even chance to a race he
acquired as chattel, and released it only under pressure? Reason
answers, never! And 10,000 prophets echo "never!" Go through the
world of history, and you will never find where two nations never
got along together. Will history now reverse itself?

We are simply battering our heads, with our eyes shut, against
a door that will never be opened. Just suppose you were imprisoned,
and that you stood, battering a door with rage, while the keeper
remained outside stolidly regarding you through the grating, when,
all at once, someone passed along, and told you that a door at the
other end was open, and you could pass through unmolested. How
great would be the joy, when you emerge to freedom! This is precisely the same thing with our race today. We are battering at the
wrong door. There stands ajar, a door though which we can pass
to a full and perfect freedom. Will we not seize the opportunity?

Here is a picture of a horse—an animal with great muscular
strength, a little child on its back, guiding it with a bit and bridle.
Does the animal know its strength? No. If it knew its power, several men could not control it. Now, a picture of a lion—an animal

with great muscular strength, and conscious of its ability to use it. Did you ever see a domesticated lion? The Negro race is like unto the horse, possessing great power, but unconscious of it. We ought to be as the lion. Know, then, ourselves! Let 400 million souls arise in unity, strength and power, and who could stay our progress? Throw aside petty jealousies, envyings, quarrels, caste, and march onward in one solid phalanx to national honor and dignity. These can be secured by no other means.

Europe, the home of the White man's civilization, has been torn to bits by the dogs of war. Her states are bankrupt, bleeding and depleted of man power. Her statesmen are apprehensive as to what the Yellow man, the Brown man, the Black man, will do. Of course, the White man naturally expects the darker races to be over docile, and help him rebuild his shattered house. We must not seek independence. You see, the White man reserve to himself the right to do certain things, which if performed by the darker races, would be almost sacrilegious. Leaving Europe, we might say, that the only strong arm of the White race is to be found in America.

In every secret society and lodge-room, the topic of a Negro nation should have a place in the "rules of order."

A central treasury should be established under competent men, from which could be drawn funds for the education of the youth of the race in navigation, civil engineering, mineral engineering, surveying and other branches which will enable us to depend on ourselves in building up a country.

Agents should be supported in every community and country, and they should be charged with the duty of educating and preparing citizens for the new Republic.

There may be some who scoff and call me visionary. Those they be that are content to stay here, and eat the crumbs that fall from the White man's table. But the thing is quite possible, were 400 million people to come together in a decision at once. Our voices would pass beyond the League of Nations, and reach the throne of Jehovah, to Whom be glory and dominion and power, for ever and ever.

Amen.

The Negro's Greatest Enemy (1923)*

Marcus Garvey

The most spectacular and the most effective of the early twentieth-century Black Nationalist leaders was a Jamaica-born Negro named Marcus Garvey. Garvey's Universal Negro Improvement Association, founded in 1914 with the slogan "Africa for the Africans, at home and abroad," acquired a following that has been estimated in the millions. Attracting his support almost entirely from the impoverished masses of the burgeoning northern ghettos, Garvey attacked light-skinned Negroes, who made up a large part of the leadership of organizations like the NAACP, as corrupted race traitors. He advocated the mass migration of American Negroes to Africa, and the eventual liberation and unification of Africa as a homeland for all Black people, and the establishment of an all-Negro religion that would teach that God and Christ were black. He urged the immediate organization of Negro-owned businesses and the UNIA-operated laundries, groceries, restaurants, and a printing plant. Garvey's most ambitious undertaking, the Black Star Steam Ship Line, was a financial disaster and led to his undoing. Pressed by traditional Negro leaders whose influence Garvey had undermined and by the governments of European nations concerned about the effect of his activities in their African colonies, the federal government tried him for mail fraud in connection with the Black Star Line. He was convicted, jailed and then deported, and the UNIA collapsed.

I was born on the island of Jamaica, British West Indies, on August 17, 1887. My parents were black Negroes. My father was a man of brilliant intellect and dashing courage. He was unafraid of consequences. He took human chances in the course of life, as most men do, and he failed at the close of his career. He once had a fortune: he died poor. My mother was a sober and conscientious Christian, too soft and good for the time in which she lived. She was the direct opposite of my father. He was severe, firm, determined, bold and strong, refusing to yield even to superior forces if he believed he was right. My mother, on the other hand, was always willing to return a smile for a blow, and ever ready to bestow charity upon her enemy. Of this strange combination I was born thirty-six years ago, and ushered into a world of sin, the flesh, and the devil.

---

* Marcus Garvey, "The Negro's Greatest Enemy," *Current History* (September, 1923), pp. 11–22.

I grew up with other Black and White boys. I was never whipped by any, but made them all respect the strength of my arms. I got my education from many sources—through private tutors, two public schools, two grammar or high schools and two colleges. My teachers were men and women of varied experiences and abilities: four of them were eminent preachers. They studied me and I studied them. With some I became friendly in after years; others and I drifted apart because as a boy they wanted to whip me, and I was not made to be whipped. It annoys me to be defeated; hence to me, to be once defeated is to find cause for an everlasting struggle to reach the top.

I became a printer's apprentice at an early age, while still attending school. My apprentice master was a highly educated and alert man. In the affairs of business and the world he had no peer. He taught me many things before I reached twelve, and at fourteen I had enough intelligence and experience to manage men. I was strong and manly, and I made them respect me. I developed a strong and forceful character, and have maintained it still.

To me, at home in my early days, there was no difference between White and Black. One of my father's properties, the place where I lived most of the time, was adjoining that of a White man. He had three girls and two boys; the Wesleyan minister, another White man whose church my parents attended, also had property adjoining ours. He had three girls and one boy. All of us were playmates. We romped and were happy children playmates together. The little White girl whom I liked most knew no better than I did myself. We were two innocent fools who never dreamed of a race feeling and problem. As a child, I went to school with White boys and girls, like all other Negroes. We were not called Negroes then. I never heard the term Negro used once until I was about fourteen.

At fourteen my little White playmate and I parted. Her parents thought the time had come to separate us and draw the color line. They sent her and another sister to Edinburgh, Scotland, and told her that she was never to write or try to get in touch with me, for I was a "nigger." It was then that I found for the first time that there was some difference in humanity, and that there were different races, each having its own separate and distinct social life. I did not care about the separation after I was told about it, because I never thought all during our childhood association that the girl and the rest of the children of her race were better than I was; in fact, they used to look up to me. So I simply had no regrets. After my first lesson in race distinction, I never thought of playing with White girls any more, even if they might be my next-door neighbors. At home my sister's company was good enough for me. White boys and I used to frolic together. We played cricket and baseball, ran races and rode bicycles together, took each other to the river and to the sea beach to learn to swim, and make boyish efforts while out in deep water to drown each other, making a sprint for shore crying out "shark, shark, shark." In all our experiences, however, only one Black boy was drowned. He went under on a Friday afternoon after school hours, and his parents found him afloat half eaten by sharks on the following Sunday afternoon. Since then we boys never went back to sea.

At maturity the Black and White boys separated, and took different courses in life. I grew up then to see the difference between the races more and more. My schoolmates as young men did not know or remember me any more. Then I realized that I had to make a fight for a place in the world, that it was not so easy to pass on to office and positions. Personally, however, I had not much difficulty in finding and holding a place for myself, for I was aggressive. At eighteen I had an excellent position as manager of a large printing establishment, having under my control several men old enough to be my grandfathers. But I got mixed up with public life. I started to take an interest in the politics of my country, and then I saw the injustice done to my race because it was Black, and I became dissatisfied on that account. I went traveling to South and Central America and parts of the West Indies to find out if it was so elsewhere, and I found the same situation. I set sail for Europe to find out if it was different there, and again I found the stumbling-block —"You are Black." I read of the conditions in America. I read *Up From Slavery*, by Booker T. Washington, and then to my doom—if I may so call it—of being a race leader dawned upon me in London after I had traveled through almost half of Europe.

I asked, "Where is the Black m..n's government?" "Where is his king and his kingdom?" "Where is his president, his country, and his ambassador, his army, his navy, his men of big affairs?" I could not find them, and then I declared, "I will help to make them."

Becoming naturally restless for the opportunity of doing something for the advancement of my race, I was determined that the Black man would not continue to be kicked about by all the other races and nations of the world, as I saw it in the West Indies, South and Central America and Europe, and as I read of it in America. My young and ambitious mind led me into flights of great imagination. I saw before me then, even as I do now, a new world of Black men, not peons, serfs, dogs and slaves, but a nation of sturdy men making their impress upon civilization and causing a new light to dawn upon the human race. I could not remain in London any more. My brain was afire. There was a world of thought to conquer. I had to start ere it became too late and the work be not done. Immediately I boarded a ship at Southampton for Jamaica, where I arrived on July 15, 1914. The Universal Negro Improvement League was founded and organized five days after my arrival, with the program of uniting all the Negro peoples of the world into one great body to establish a country and government absolutely their own.

Where did the name of the organization come from? It was while speaking to a West Indian Negro who was a passenger on the ship with me from Southampton, who was returning home to the West Indies from Basutoland with his Basuto wife, that I further learned of the horrors of native life in Africa. He related to me in conversation such horrible and pitiable tales that my heart bled within me. Retiring from the conversation to my cabin, all day and the following night I pondered over the subject matter of that conversation, and at midnight, lying flat on my back, the vision and thought came to me that I should name the organization the Universal Negro Improvement Association and African Communities (Imperial) League. Such a name I thought would embrace the purpose of all Black humanity. Thus to the world a name was born, a movement created, and a man became known.

I really never knew there was so much color prejudice in Jamaica, my own native home, until I started the work of the Universal Negro Improvement Association. We started immediately before the war. I had just returned from a successful trip to Europe, which was an exceptional achievement for a Black man. The daily papers wrote me up with big headlines and told of my movement. But nobody wanted to be a Negro. "Garvey is crazy; he has lost his head." "Is that the use he is going to make of his experience and intelligence?"—such were the criticisms passed upon me. Men and women as black as I, and even more so, had believed themselves White under the West Indian order of society. I was simply an impossible man to use openly the term "Negro"; yet every one beneath his breath was calling the Black man a Negro.

I had to decide whether to please my friends and be one of the "black Whites" of Jamaica, and be reasonably prosperous, or come out openly and defend and help improve and protect the integrity of the black millions and suffer. I decided to do the latter, hence my offense against "Colored-Black-White" society in the colonies and America. I was openly hated and persecuted by some of these Colored men of the island who did not want to be classified as Negroes, but as White. They hated me worse than poison. They opposed me at every step, but I had a large number of White friends who encouraged and helped me. Notable among them were the then Governor of the Colony, the Colonial Secretary and several other prominent men. But they were afraid of offending the "Colored gentry" that were passed for White. Hence my fight had to be made alone. I spent hundreds of pounds (sterling) helping the organization to gain a footing. I also gave up all my time to the promulgation of its ideals. I became a marked man, but I was determined that the work should be done.

The war helped a great deal in arousing the consciousness of the Colored people to the reasonableness of our program, especially after the British at home had rejected a large number of Wst Indies Colored men who wanted to be officers in the British army. When they were told that Negroes could not be officers in the British army they started their own propaganda, which supplemented the program of the Universal Negro Improvement Association. With this and other contributing agencies a few of the stiff-necked Colored people began to see the reasonableness of my program, but they were firm in refusing to be known as Negroes. Furthermore, I was a Black man and therefore had absolutely no right to lead; in the opinion of the "Colored" element, leadership should have been in the hands of a Yellow or a very light man. On such flimsy prejudices our race has been retarded. There is more bitterness among us Negroes because of the caste of color than there is between any other peoples, not excluding the people of India.

I succeeded to a great extent in establishing the association in Jamaica with the assistance of a Catholic Bishop, the Governor, Sir John Pringle, the Reverend William Graham, a Scottish clergyman, and several other White friends. I got in touch with Booker Washington and told him what I wanted to do. He invited me to America and promised to speak with me in the southern and other States to help my work. Although he died in the fall of 1915, I made my arrangements and arrived in the United States on March 23, 1916.

Here I found a new and different problem. I immediately visited some of the then-called Negro leaders, only to discover, after a close study of them, that they had no program but were mere opportunists who were living off their so-called leadership while the poor people were groping in the dark. I traveled through thirty-eight states and everywhere found the same condition. I visited Tuskegee and paid my respects to the dead hero, Booker Washington, and then returned to New York, where I organized the New York division of the Universal Negro Improvement Association. After instructing the people in the aims and objects of the association, I intended returning to Jamaica to perfect the Jamaica organization, but when we had enrolled about 800 or 1,000 members in the Harlem district and had elected the officers a few Negro politicians began trying to turn the movement into a political club.

Seeing that these politicians were about to destroy my ideals, I had to fight to get them out of the organization. There it was that I made my first political enemies in Harlem. They fought me until they smashed the first organization and reduced its membership to about fifty. I started again, and in two months built up a new organization of about 1,500 members. Again the politicians came and divided us into two factions. They took away all the books of the organization, its treasury and all its belongings. At that time I was only an organizer, for it was not then my intention to remain in America, but to return to Jamaica. The organization had its proper officers elected, and I was not an officer of the New York division, but president of the Jamaica branch.

On the second split in Harlem thirteen of the members conferred with me and requested me to become president for a time of the New York organization so as to save them from the politicians. I consented and was elected president. There then sprung up two factions, one led by the politicians with the books and the money, and the other led by me. My faction had no money. I placed at their disposal what money I had, opened an office for them, rented a meeting place, employed two women secretaries, went on the streets of Harlem at night to speak for the movement. In three weeks more then 2,000 new members joined. By this time I had the association incorporated so as to prevent the other faction using the name, but in two weeks the politicians had stolen all the people's money and had smashed up their faction.

The organization under my presidency grew by leaps and bounds. I started *The Negro World*. Being a journalist, I edited this paper free of cost for the association, and worked for them without pay until November, 1920. I traveled all over the country for the association at my own expense, and established branches until in 1919 we had about thirty branches in different cities. By my writings and speeches we were able to build up a large organization of over 2 million by June, 1919, at which time we launched the program of the Black Star Line.

To have built up a new organization which was not purely political among Negroes in America was a wonderful feat, for the Negro politician does not allow any other kind of organization within his race to thrive. We succeeded, however, in making the Universal Negro Improvement Association so formidable in 1919 that we encountered more trouble from our political brethren. They sought the influence of the district attorney's office of the county of New York to put us out of business. Edwin P. Kilroe, at that time an assistant district attorney, on the complaint of the Negro politicians, started to investigate us and the association. Mr. Kilroe would constantly and continuously call me to his office for investigation on extraneous matters without coming to the point. The result was that after the eighth or ninth time I wrote an article in our newspaper, *The Negro World,* against him. This was interpreted as a criminal libel, for which I was indicted and arrested but subsequently dismissed on retracting what I had written.

During my tilts with Mr. Kilroe, the question of the Black Star Line was discussed. He did not want us to have a line of ships. I told him that even as there was a White Star Line, we would have, irrespective of his wishes, a Black Star Line. On June 27, 1919, we incorporated the Black Star Line of Delaware, and in September we obtained a ship.

The following month [October] a man by the name of Tyler came to my office at 56 West 135th Street, New York City, and told me that Mr. Kilroe had sent him to "get me," and at once fired four shots at me from a .38-caliber revolver. He wounded me in the right leg and the right side of my scalp. I was taken to the Harlem Hospital, and he was arrested. The next day it was reported that he committed suicide in jail just before he was to be taken before a city magistrate.

The first year of our activities for the Black Star Line added prestige to the Universal Negro Improvement Association. Several hundred thousand dollars' worth of shares were sold. Our first ship, the steamship *Yarmouth,* had made two voyages to the West Indies and Central America. The White press had flashed the news all over the world. I, a young Negro, as president of the corporation, had become famous. My name was discussed on five continents. The Universal Negro Improvement Association gained millions of followers all over the world. By August, 1920, over 4 million persons had joined the movement. A convention of all the Negro peoples of the world was called to meet in New York that month. Delegates came from all parts of the known world. Over 25,000 persons packed the Madison Square Garden on August 1 to hear me speak to the first International Convention of Negroes. It was a record-breaking meeting, the first and the biggest of its kind. The name of Garvey had become known as a leader of his race.

Such fame among Negroes was too much for other race leaders and politicians to tolerate. My downfall was planned by my enemies. They laid all kinds of traps for me. They scattered their spies among the employees of the Black Star Line and the Universal Negro Improvement Association. Our office records were stolen. Employees started to be openly dishonest; we could get no convictions against them; even if on complaint they were held by a magistrate, they were dismissed by the Grand Jury. The ships' officers started to pile up thousands of dollars of debts against the company without the knowledge of the officers of the corporation. Our ships were damaged at sea, and there was a general riot of wreck and ruin. Officers of the Universal Negro Improvement Association also began to steal and be openly dishonest. I had to dismiss them. They joined my enemies, and thus I had an endless fight on my hands to save the ideals of the association and carry out our program for the race. My Negro enemies, finding that they alone could not destroy me, resorted to misrepresenting me to the leaders of the White race, several of whom, without proper investigation, also opposed me.

With robberies from within and from without, the Black Star Line was forced to suspend active business in December, 1921. While I was on a business trip to the West Indies in the spring of 1921, the Black Star Line received the blow from which it was unable to recover. A sum of $25,000 was paid by one of the officers of the corporation to a man to purchase a ship, but the ship was never obtained and the money was never returned. The company was defrauded of a further sum of $11,000. Through such actions on the part of dishonest men in the shipping business the Black Star Line received its first setback. This resulted in my being indicted for using the United States mail to defraud investors in the company. I was subsequently convicted and sentenced to five years in a federal penitentiary. My trial is a matter of history. I know I was not given a square deal, because my indictment was the result of a "frame-up" among my political and business enemies. I had to conduct my own case in court because of the peculiar position in which I found myself. I had millions of friends and a large number of enemies. I wanted a Colored attorney to handle my case, but there was none I could trust. I feel that I have been denied justice because of prejudice. Yet I have an abundance of faith in the courts of America, and I hope yet to obtain justice on my appeal.

The temporary ruin of the Black Star Line has in no way affected the larger work of the Universal Negro Improvement Association, which now has 900 branches with an approximate membership of 6 million. This organization had succeeded in organizing the Negroes all over the world and we now look forward to a renaissance that will create a new people and bring about the restoration of Ethiopia's ancient glory.

Being Black, I have committed an unpardonable offense against the very light-colored Negroes in America and the West Indies by making myself famous as a Negro leader of millions. In their view, no Black man must rise above them, but I still forge ahead determined to give to the world the truth about the new Negro who is determined to make and hold for himself a place in the affairs of men. The Universal Negro Improvement Association has been misrepresented by my enemies. They have tried to make it appear that we are hostile to other races. This is absolutely false. We love all humanity. We are working for the peace of the world which we believe can only come about when all races are given their due.

We feel that there is absolutely no reason why there should be any differences between the Black and White races, if each stop to adjust and steady itself. We believe in the purity of both races. We do not believe the Black man should be encouraged in the idea that his highest purpose in life is to marry a White woman, but we do believe that the White man should be taught to respect the Black woman in the same way as he wants the Black man to respect the White woman. It is a vicious and dangerous doctrine of social equality to urge, as certain Colored leaders do, that Black and White should get together, for that would destroy the racial purity of both.

We believe that the Black people should have a country of their own where they should be given the fullest opportunity to develop politically, socially and industrially. The Black people should not be encouraged to remain in White people's countries and expect to be presidents, governors, mayors, senators, congressman, judges, and social and industrial leaders. We believe that with the rising ambition of the Negro, if a country is not provided for him in another fifty or a hundred years, there will be a terrible clash that will end disastrously to him and disgrace our civilization. We desire to prevent such a clash by pointing the Negro to a home of his own. We feel that all well disposed and broadminded White men will aid in this direction. It is because of this belief no doubt that my Negro enemies, so as to prejudice me further in the opinion of the public, wickedly state that I am a member of the Ku Klux Klan, even though I am a Black man.

I have been deprived of the opportunity of properly explaining my work to the White people of America through the prejudice worked up against me by jealous and wicked members of my own race. My success as an organizer was much more than rival Negro leaders could tolerate. They, regardless of consequences either to me or to the race, had to destroy me by fair means or foul. The thousands of anonymous and other hostile letters written to the editors and publishers of the White press by Negro rivals to prejudice me in the eyes of public opinion are sufficient evidence of the wicked and vicious opposition I have had to meet from among my own people, especially among the very light-colored. But they went further than the press in their attempts to discredit me. They organized clubs all over the United States and the West Indies, and wrote both open and anonymous letters to city, state, and federal officials of this and other governments to induce them to use their influence to hamper and destroy me. No wonder, therefore, that several judges, district attorneys, and other high officials have been against me without knowing me. No wonder, therefore, that the great White population of this country and of the world has a wrong impression of the aims, and objects of the Universal Negro Improvement Association . . . and of the work of Marcus Garvey.

Having had the wrong education as a start in his racial career, the Negro has become his own greatest enemy. Most of the trouble I have had in advancing the cause of the race has come from Negroes. Booker Washington aptly described the race in one of his lectures by stating that we were like crabs in a barrel, that none would allow the other to climb over, but on any such attempt all would continue to pull back into the barrel the one crab that would make the effort to climb out. Yet, those of us with vision cannot desert the race, leaving it to suffer and die.

Looking forward a century or two, we can see an economic and political death struggle for the survival of the different race groups. Many of our present-day national centers will have become overcrowded with vast surplus populations. The fight for bread and position will be keen and severe. The Association, we are fighting for the founding of a Negro nation in Africa, so that there will be no clash between Black and White and that each race will have a separate existence and . . . civilization all its own without courting suspicion and hatred or eyeing each other with jealousy and rivalry within the borders of the same country.

White men who have struggled for and built up their countries and their own civilizations are not disposed to hand them over to the Negro or any other race without let or hindrance. It would be unreasonable to expect this. Hence any vain assumption on the part of a Negro to imagine that he will one day become president of the nation, governor of the state, or mayor of the city in the countries of White men, is like waiting on the devil and his angels to take up their residence in the Realm on High and direct there the affairs of paradise.

The Only Way to Redeem Africa (1923)*

A. Philip Randolph

A. Philip Randolph, founder in 1919 of the influential radical magazine, *The Messenger*, and in the mid-1920's of the Brotherhood of Sleeping Car Porters (the most powerful Negro labor organization), advocated Marxism as the solution for the problems faced by the Negro in the 1920's. In the following article, he attacked Marcus Garvey's movement as a barrier to the development of international working-class solidarity, which alone, he argued, could emancipate Africa and the American Negro by overthrowing capitalism.

Of course, there is nothing more normal and logical than that the idea of building up a Negro empire should flow from the "Back to Africa" Movement. A word about the difficulties to be overcome. First, with the opposition of the White Powers, it would not even be feasible for the Garvey crowd to even land in Africa. Second, granting that they were allowed to land, they would have nothing to conquer Africa with, for it is not conceivable that Great Britain, France, Italy, or America would supply their foe with the means for overthrowing their own dominion anywhere; and there is no spot in Africa where a landing can be effected which is not controlled by a great White power. In Africa, three obstacles would have to be overcome by the Garvey group: namely, the great White powers, the natives who are opposed to alien rule, and nature in Africa, such as the intensely hot tropical climate, the uncultivated soil, the wild beasts and deadly reptiles, together with a forbidding forest. *Neither one of these three obstacles could a group of uneducated, unarmed, and unorganized Negroes—such as the Garvey crew— overcome.*

In view of the foregoing difficulties, it ought to be clear to the most Africoid-Negro Garveyite that it would require unlimited technical, scientific skill, and knowledge, together with billions of dollars of capital to subdue, harness up, and develop the nature aspect of Africa alone, to say nothing of driving out the entrenched

---

* From A. Philip Randolph, "The Only Way to Redeem Africa," *The Messenger*, V (1923), 568–570, 612–614.

White powers and subjecting the intractable natives. *Conquering Africa is not any less difficult than conquering Europe.*

Thus, I think that we are justified in asking the question, that if Mr. Garvey is seriously interested in establishing a Negro nation why doesn't he begin with Jamaica, West Indies (*not Jamaica, Long Island*). Jamaica is but a small island with a population of 850,000—the White population consisting of less than 20,000. Obviously, on a small island where the ratio of Black and White inhabitants is 42 to 1, the Negroes ought to be able to overcome the Whites and establish control. Then, too, Jamaica is Mr. Garvey's home. He ought to know the geography of the island, the language, and customs of the people. In other words, he is far better qualified to establish a Negro nation in Jamaica than he is in Africa—a land which he has never visited, of the customs and language of whose inhabitants he is entirely ignorant. Besides, I submit that it is much easier to overthrow one White power such as controls Jamaica, than it is to overthrow six White powers equipped with the greatest armies and navies the world has ever known, such as control Africa. And, too, it requires much less capital, less brains, less power. Don't you think Jamaica is the logical place for Mr. Garvey to begin his plans for establishing a Negro nation?

There is also Liberia who tried to sell her independence to the investment bankers of America for a loan of $5 million. If Mr. Garvey is so interested in a Negro nation, why didn't he come to the rescue of Liberia, by raising $5 million, to save her from being gobbled up by the American imperialistic eagle. *No, he didn't do that but responsible persons say that he raised money presumably as a loan for a redemption fund for Liberia and that only an insignificant part of it was ever used in the interest of Liberia.* As an evidence of the thought which Liberia gave the Garvey movement, when President King of Liberia was in the United States seeking a loan of $5 million, he never had the slightest association in any way with the Garvey outfit. Besides, Haiti is a struggling Black nation which needs help. *Why doesn't Mr. Garvey expel the United States from Haiti?* Here is a Black people who won their liberty over a hundred years ago. Now they are under the imperial heel of the United States. Why doesn't Brother Marcus help keep a Negro nation independent instead of trying to build up a new one?

For if a Negro nation is all he wants, then he has two: Liberia and Haiti.

But granting that it were possible to establish a Black empire in Africa, it would not be desirable. *Black despotism is as objectionable as white despotism.* A Black landlord is no more sympathetic with Black tenants than White landlords are. A Negro is no more interested in having his pocketbook stolen by a Black thief than he is in having it stolen by a White thief. Death is no sweeter at the hands of a Black murderer than it is at the hands of a White murderer.

Again, empires are passing. Witness Russia, Germany and Austria-Hungary. Garvey has begun empire-building too late. Even Germany started in the empire business too late. She wanted to build a *Mittel Europa* from Berlin to Bagdad, but she was thwarted. Great Britain, France, Italy, and Russia of the Czar were not interested in having any more competitors in the empire business. Hence they crushed her. Such would be the fate of an African empire, granting that one could be established. It is also of special moment to note that no people love empires save the ruling class who live by the exploitation of the subject or working class. Such was the reason for the revolt of the Russian people against the Russian empire. *The ruling and subject classes were both White, but that did not keep back the revolution.* Note also the revolutions in Germany and Austria-Hungary, and the revolt in Ireland, India, and Korea against empire rule. Then there is Mexico under Diaz. Oppression produces revolutions whether in White or Black empires. *Thus, an African empire would last no longer than the African workers became conscious of oppression and their power to remove it, and then, they would overthrow and decapitate a Black king as quickly as they would overthrow and decapitate a White king.*

In harmony with the "Back to Africa", "anti-White man" and "Negro First" doctrines, the Black Star Line, the Red Star Line, etc., Mr. Garvey never took any thought of the existing monopoly in the shipping business, the need of hundreds of millions of capital, banking houses to manipulate international exchange, as well as the necessity of having experts in the shipping game to handle the business. The absence of either one of these indispensables would spell failure to any shipping project, and needless to say that Mr.

Marcus neither had nor has either. Think of the Black Star Line competing in maritime affairs when the United States government is compelled to subsidize the United States [Merchant] Marine. It is difficult to make the shipping business pay when operated by the best brains with unlimited capital. *What will the Black Star Line do without brains or capital?* Negroes can no more expect to succeed in the shipping business than they can hope to succeed in the subway or telephone or gas business in New York City, or in the railroad business between New York and Chicago or New York and Washington, D.C. *These are monopolies that cannot thrive were duplication or competition exists. It is sheer folly to talk of building a ship line to transport Negroes only.* Not enough Negroes travel to Africa, the West Indies—*or to anywhere for that matter*—to support such an enterprise.

It would appear, then that Mr. Garvey is not so much concerned about the soundness, feasibility, or value of a project as he is about getting together something that will duplicate the efforts and works of the Whites. As fortune or misfortune would have it, he always selects the most impossible things among the Whites to imitate. His policy is to run the entire gamut of slavish imitation from empire building, ship lines, a Black House in Washington, D.C., a Black Cross Nurse, a Provisional President with a Royal Court (little different this, eh?). *Presidents don't have courts, it's the pastime of kings; but what's that ridiculous contradiction to the "Most Dishonorable," etc.?*

The Garveyites are so strong on imitation that they attempt to justify the Black Star Line disgrace by pointing to the millions of dollars that the United States Shipping Board lost. *In other words, if a White man takes arsenic, a Negro ought to take it too.* A sort of getting-even policy, with the Negroes always the victim. *Think of Negroes competing in losing money with the United States government, which has the power to tax both White and Black to raise revenue.*

If Mr. Garvey was competing for the first prize for producing the largest number of failures among Negroes, he would win with hands down. All his efforts are of a piece with the Black Star Line in practicality. As fast as one little, dirty, mismanaged, junk grocery store fails, he starts another one in his senseless efforts to compete with James Butler, Andrew Davey, the Atlantic & Pacific

Tea Co., and Daniel Reeves, the largest chain store systems in the world, operating with hundreds of millions of capital and the greatest business experts in their time.

In order to inveigle the enthusiastic but uncritical, the Brother proceeds from one pipe-dream to another, calling for each and every Negro of the 400 millions in the world, (*remember it's not one more and not one less*) to slip from one to one hundred beans into his various schemes, and new ones are always in the making. Note the Booker T. Washington University, if you please, the *Negro Daily Times*, the Phyllis Wheatley Hotel, the Universal Publishing House. These gestures are intended to impress the Garvey fanatics with the idea that they are owned by the UNIA, that they represent great business strides of the organization, so that they will not be unwilling to dig down into their jeans again for more cash to drop into the Garvey bottomless money pits. *It is too evident that the running of the* Negro Daily Times *will rival the Black Star Line in not running.* It is well that the Negro is not fated to depend upon this *Times* to find out the *time* of the happening of anything. They will not be able to even buy the paper, to say nothing about printing it. And, of course, the Booker T. Washington University is mere moonshine. It will have neither students nor teachers. *Students will not trust it to give out knowledge; nor will teachers trust it to give out pay.*

But if there were any grounds of reality to his rabid, sensational, theatrical, kaleidoscopic blandishments, then Brother Garvey ought to be able to operate some of the *smaller* things, at least.

For instance, if he actually had 4.5 million members in his organization, paying dues of 40 cents a month, he would have a revenue of $1.8 million per month or $21 million a year. But it is obvious that if he were getting that revenue, it would not be necessary for the *Yarmouth,* a ship for which the UNIA paid the handsome sum of $145,000, and upon which, according to Mr. Garvey testifying in the Seventh Municipal District Court, they had lost $300,000 on its first voyage, to be sold at auction by the United States Marshal on December 2, 1921, for the pitiful sum of $1,625. Nor would it be necessary for the organization to be constantly sued for wages by its employees.

It would certainly be unnecessary for Brother Marcus to end his weekly front-page braying with constant begging for the where-

withal with which to run the convention, the 101 different slippery
jokers, and incidentally himself. Thus, the only logical conclusion
is that the dear Brother is either a consummate liar or a notorious
crook. If he were getting $21.6 million a year from 4.5 million mem-
bers, certainly he would not be constantly pressed into the courts
by enraged creditors; if he is not getting it, he is lying about the
membership of the UNIA, the only motive I can assign for which
is that he has a mania for wanting to appear as a great man—a
man who could organize 4.5 million Negroes.

But his membership is about as real as the number of delegates
who attended his convention. He advertised 150,000 delegates would
be at the convention. Responsible delegates at the convention state
that there were not more than 300. According to this mountebank,
15,000 Negro preachers alone would attend. A canvass of the delegates disclosed that not a single responsible, respectable, intelligent
Negro preacher in America was at the convention. Hence, a sound
policy for one to adopt is to accept with a grain of salt everything
that emanates from that "Temple of Annanias" in 138th Street,
New York.

It is just that irresponsible method of misrepresentation and
exaggeration of Mr. Garvey's that is expressing itself in a vicious
policy which introduces dissension and suspicion as between Blacks
and mulattoes. Still this is in harmony with his "Back to Africa"
idea out of which the "anti-White man's" doctrine grows; for if it
be a sound policy to oppose all White men, then it follows, as night
the day, that it is also a sound policy to oppose everything which
possesses any of the so-called White man's blood. How foolish, how
vicious! If such inanity gained much headway in America, it would
well-nigh wreck every Negro home, setting brother against sister
and husband against wife.

Yet even the dividing of the Negro into shades of color does not
complete the vicious circle of Garveyism. Perhaps the "most un-
kindest of all" is the fostering of intraracial prejudices such as
color and nationality. Still it is not unnatural that nationality prejudice should spring from the "Back to Africa" bogey. Why? If
Negroes are bent upon going back to Africa, they will not prepare
to remain in America; and, if they don't plan to remain here, they
will not strive to acquire rights and privileges, economic and social
or political; they will not fight groups or forces that would seek to

deny them such rights. *In fact, they will combine with agencies that desire to get rid of the Negro.* Such is the logical "Back to Africa" reason for Garvey's alliance with the Ku Klux Klan. Of course, there may have been other reasons, and doubtless there were.

Now, it is a matter of common knowledge that the Ku Klux Klan is the historic enemy of the American Negro. It was organized to destroy Negro suffrage, to re-enslave him. It murdered, burned up and lynched thousands of innocent, defenseless Negroes. Southern Negroes with a spark of manhood in them, would suffer their tongues to be torn from their mouths before they would dare to give any color of support to this band of criminal, cut-throat bandits. Yet Mr. Garvey found it necessary to hold a secret interview with the King Kleagle Clarke (an interview, by the way, which he promised to publish, but which has not yet seen the light of publicity) after which he had the unmitigated effrontery to come before the American Negroes and advise them not to fight the Klan. He says it is not an alliance. But note this illustration: During the war if anyone in America had advised anyone else not to fight Germany, what would he have been considered as? Obviously, a spy—an ally of Germany. Certainly he would have been recognized as the enemy of America. So it is with Mr. Garvey. *He has joined the enemy of the American Negro, and, consequently, can only be considered as the enemy of the the American Negro.* But you ask what relation has this to prejudice between the American and West Indian Negro? This: Mr. Garvey is a West Indian. As the leader of the Universal Negro Improvement Association, it is assumed that the followers endorse his policies. It is also assumed by American Negroes, wrongly, of course, that all West Indians are followers of Garvey. Thus, the deduction of the American Negro is that all West Indians, like Garvey, are their enemy. While this is not true, it is believed to be true; and people act more strongly upon belief than they do upon fact and truth. The most prominent, intelligent West Indians are opposing Garvey. Garvey does not represent all West Indians any more than did Booker T. Washington represent all American Negroes.

Again, Mr. Garvey, as a symbol to his followers, holds up a non-citizenship policy, which is a logical result of the "Back to Africa" tommyrot. No one plans to vote in a place which he is going to leave. When I am in Philadelphia, I don't plan to vote because I don't intend to remain there. So it is with anyone who looks upon the place at which he happens to be as a temporary abode, from which he is soon to leave for his permanent home.

But, while this attitude of mind obtains among the Garveyites, it does not obtain among the American Negroes. Still, Mr. Garvey pretends to represent all of the Negroes of the world! Thus, outsiders would assume that the policy of Garvey's is accepted by the American Negro, too. This, of course, is not true. Mr. Garvey only represents the views of ignorant West Indian and American Negroes. Now the American Negro views the Garvey non-citizenship policy as a menace to himself, and rightly so. *For anyone who presumes to speak for the American Negro, whose problem is largely political, and ignores and repudiates citizenship by refusing to become a citizen himself, demoralizes the political struggles of the American Negro.* Again American Negroes believe that all West Indians are non-citizens. It does not matter that this is not true, it is regarded as true, and that is all that counts. It can not be expected that the average American Negro will make a distinction between Garvey and the rank-and-file West Indians any more than it could have been expected that the American people would have made a distinction between the Kaiser and the German people, although we knew that there were Germans who opposed the war policies of the Kaiser.

Garvey's non-citizenship policy is unsound. I am not considering the element of citizenship from any abstract point of view. Citizenship in the United States is no better than citizenship in Great Britain, France, or Russia. The question is not the rightness or wrongness of becoming a citizen. The intrinsic value *per se,* is not an issue. The only question is, *does it or does it not invest one with certain advantages?* It is purely a matter of gain, of profit, of benefit to the West Indian, or for that matter, to any foreigner. If the West Indian Negro would or would not participate in the solution of the Negro problem in America, it would be in his interest to become a citizen. Nor would I maintain that the West Indian Negro hasn't the right to essay a solution of the Negro problem in America merely because he is a foreigner. As I said before, it is not a question of the abstract right of a foreigner to work for the solution of certain problems, but the question is how much more effectively may he not attack the problem as a citizen than he can as a foreigner. *The very fact that one is a worker invests him with the fundamental right to deal with everything, wherever he is, that relates to his struggle for a living.* It is to his interest, at all times, to adopt every method calculated to improve his position as a worker, and if he suffers from other disabilities such as race, then it is the part of wisdom for him to employ such policies as will assure him a greater measure of racial justice.

Now, it is recognized that political power makes legislation and that legislation can modify the social and economic life of groups for good or ill. It is also a matter of general understanding that political power can only be acquired by meeting the conditions of citizenship. It is also elementary that whether one be a citizen or not, he is affected by the legislation of the country where he happens to be residing. *Thus, upon the basis of enlightened self-interest, the West Indian Negro should meet the conditions of citizenship in order that he may acquire political power with which to protect and advance his own economic and social life and also to increase the political power of the Negro group in the United States of America, which would go farther toward improving the condition of the Negro in Africa, Haiti, and the West Indies than a thousand UNIA's.* Thus Garvey's blustering talk about citizenship in Africa at the sacrifice of citizenship in America is a decidedly pernicious example.

Witness the attitude of the Jews. They know an advantage when they see one. They immediately become citizens and employ their political power to assist their plan to build up a Jewish home in Palestine. But, of course, no Jewish leader advocates any "Back to Palestine" slogan. Nor do they build any Jewish steamship lines, or Jewish House in Washington, D. C. Still the Jews have their problems here and elsewhere. No Jew would drop so low as to join the Klan, and especially, no leader.

What is true of the Jews is also true of the Irish. They never fail to exercise their political power, which means they never fail to become naturalized. Nor do the Irish propagate any "back to Ireland" doctrines. They build no Irish shiplines and establish no "Irish Houses" in the capitals of various nations.

Mr. Marcus finds himself as the greatest vaudeville comedian in Christendom. His organization is neither large nor sound; it is merely funny. But even if it were a large group, it would prove nothing. Mere organization is not material. The issue is the kind of organization, its purpose. The Klan is an organization but no sane person would praise the Imperial Wizard Simmons as a great man from the point of view of benefit he brought to the people. And no sensible person considers greatness from any other point of view save that of benefit to some department of human life.

A word now about tearing down that which has been built up.

It is maintained by some that it is wrong to tear down, that it is against the interest of the Negro. Let us see. In order to settle this point, it is necessary to determine the character of the thing which one proposes to tear down. Destruction is as essential as construction. For example, the foundation of a house can not be laid until the debris has been removed, excavation effected. They also argue that one should not tear down anything until he has something else to put in its place. That is not correct thinking. No one would contend that smallpox germs should not be destroyed until some other germs are discovered to be put in their place. No, not at all. When once the smallpox germs are destroyed, a condition is set up that will permit the human body to begin re-establishing sound health. The same principle of action holds good with respect to social health. *The Garvey Movement is a social-racial disease germ to the Negro, which must be destroyed in order that he may proceed to build up a powerful organization to protect his interests.* Of course, there exist Negro organizations that are committed to constructive policies. There are the Friends of Negro Freedom and the National Association for the Advancement of Colored People, the former presenting a social-economic program, the latter a civil program.

Now as to the remedy for the redemption of Africa.

First, the cause of the African question is world imperialism. Africa is exploited just as China, the Philippines, Haiti, Cuba, Korea, Ireland, India are exploited. The issue is not race, color, or nationality, but economics. Africa is held in subjection because it is the home of rubber, gold, diamonds, cocoa, kernels, iron, coal, etc. These raw materials are necessary to the western capitalist European and American powers. The investment bankers send millions of dollars into these underdeveloped countries, and in order to protect the said investments, huge navies and armies are built up and maintained. Militarism, the handmaiden of financial imperialism, is developed to insure the safety of the Western European and American powers' economic spheres of influence, where labor is cheap, raw materials plentiful, and, consequently, the return on capital high.

The method of imperialism consists in making loans to certain tribal chieftains, heads of weak governments, such as Morocco, Egypt, Haiti, Santa Domingo, Liberia, China, India, etc. When the default in payments is made, the great power steps in and establishes control. Africa then will never be free so long as financial imperialism holds sway in society, and financial imperialism will hold dominion just so long as the resources and means of wealth, production, and exchange are privately owned. As long as surplus wealth is created in the capitalist countries of the world, that wealth will be invested in countries where the profits are high, and one of those countries happens to be Africa. So long as investments are made in Africa or China, neither Africa nor China can be free, because whoever controls the economic power will control the social and political power. *Thus the problem consists in overthrowing capitalism.* Of course, this is an ultimate matter. For the present, only reforms can be adopted which may improve the status of the Africans. For instance, the abolition of forced labor, the retention of fertile land for the African for his own cultivation, the recognition of tribal policy, the establishment of an International Commission composed of African, American, West Indian, South and Central American Negroes, together with certain experts, White or Black, to study African life, language, customs, culture, traditions, history, etc., in order that it may make reports upon which constructive social, economic, and political policies of reform may be based. *Such is the only way to redeem Africa, Mr. Marcus Garvey to the contrary notwithstanding.*

Soviet Russia and the Negro (1923)*

Claude McKay

During the 1920's and 1930's many American Negroes were influenced by the ideals of the Russian Revolution. The Communist call for the revolutionary liberation of oppressed and colonialized peoples throughout the world had a particularly strong attraction for black intellectuals in Asia, Africa and Latin America. A number of prominent Negro artists and writers joined or sympathized with the Communist movement. Richard Wright and Ralph Ellison, outstanding Negro authors, have described their attraction to and eventual disillusionment with the Soviet influenced American Communist Party. Claude McKay, one of the young poets and novelists who contributed to the literary and artistic movement of the 1920's that has been called the "Harlem Renaissance," here describes the impact of a visit to the Soviet Union in the early years after the Bolshevik Revolution.

The world upheaval having brought the three greatest European nations England, France and Germany—into closer relationship with Negroes, Colored Americans should seize the opportunity to promote finer interracial understanding. As White Americans in Europe are taking advantage of the situation to intensify their propaganda against the Blacks, so must Negroes meet that with a strong counter-movement. Negroes should realize that the supremacy of American capital today proportionately increases American influence in the politics and social life of the world. Every American official abroad, every smug tourist is a protagonist of dollar culture and a propagandist against the Negro. Besides brandishing the Rooseveltian stick in the face of the lesser new world natives, America holds an economic club over the heads of all the great European nations, excepting Russia, and so those bold individuals in Western Europe who formerly sneered at dollar culture may yet find it necessary and worth while to be discreetly silent. As American influence increases in the world, and especially in Europe, through the extension of American capital, the more necessary it becomes for all struggling minorities of the United States to organize extensively for the world wide propagation of their griev-

* Claude McKay, "Soviet Russia and the Negro," *The Crisis* (December, 1923), 61–65.

ances. Such propaganda efforts, besides strengthening the cause at home, will certainly enlist the sympathy and help of those foreign groups that are carrying on a life and death struggle to escape the octuple arms of American business interests. And the Negro, as the most suppressed and persecuted minority, should use this period of ferment in international affairs to lift his cause out of his national obscurity and force it forward as a prime international issue.

Though western Europe can be reported as being quite ignorant and apathetic of the Negro in world affairs, there is one great nation with an arm in Europe that is thinking intelligently on the Negro as it does about all international problems. When the Russian workers overturned their infamous government in 1917, one of the first acts of the new premier, Lenin, was a proclamation greeting all the oppressed peoples throughout the world, exhorting them to organize and unite against the common international oppressor—private capitalism. Later on in Moscow, Lenin himself grappled with the question of the American Negroes and spoke on the subject before the Second Congress of the Third International. He consulted with John Reed, the American journalist, and dwelt on the urgent necessity of propaganda and organizational work among the Negroes of the South. The subject was not allowed to drop. When Sen Katayama of Japan, the veteran revolutionist, went from the United States to Russia in 1921 he placed the American Negro problem first upon his full agenda. And ever since he has been working unceasingly and unselfishly to promote the cause of the exploited American Negro among the Soviet councils of Russia.

With the mammoth country securely under their control, and despite the great energy and thought that are being poured into the revival of the national industry, the vanguard of the Russian workers and the national minorities, now set free from imperial oppression, are thinking seriously about the fate of the oppressed classes, the suppressed national and racial minorities in the rest of Europe, Asia, Africa, and America. They feel themselves kin in spirit to these people. They want to help make them free. And not the least of the oppressed that fill the thoughts of the new Russia are the Negroes of America and Africa. If we look back two decades to recall how the Czarist persecution of the Russian Jews agitated democratic America, we will get some idea of the mind of liberated

Russia towards the Negroes of America. The Russian people are reading the terrible history of their own recent past in the tragic position of the American Negro today. Indeed, the southern states can well serve the purpose of showing what has happened in Russia. For if the exploited poor Whites of the South could ever transform themselves into making common cause with the persecuted and plundered Negroes, overcome the oppressive oligarchy—the political crackers and robber landlords—and deprive it of all political privileges, the situation would be very similar to that of Soviet Russia today.

In Moscow I met an old Jewish revolutionist who had done time in Siberia, now young again and filled with the spirit of the triumphant Revolution. We talked about American affairs and touched naturally on the subject of the Negro. I told him of the difficulties of the problem, that the best of the liberal White elements were also working for a better status for the Negro, and he remarked: "When the democratic bourgeoisie of the United States were execrating Czardom for the Jewish pogroms they were meting out to your people a treatment more savage and barbarous than the Jews ever experienced in the old Russia. America, he said religiously,

> had to make some sort of expiatory gesture for her sins. There is no surfeited bourgeoisie here in Russia to make a hobby of ugly social problems, but the Russian workers, who have won through the ordeal of persecution and revolution, extend the hand of international brotherhood to all the suppressed Negro millions of America.

I met with this spirit of sympathetic appreciation and response prevailing in all circles in Moscow and Petrograd. I never guessed what was awaiting me in Russia. I had left America in September of 1922 determined to get here, to see into the new revolutionary life of the people and report on it. I was not a little dismayed when, congenitally averse to notoriety as I am, I found that on stepping upon Russian soil I forthwith became a notorious character. And strangely enough there was nothing unpleasant about my being swept into the surge of revolutionary Russia. For better or for worse every person in Russia is vitally affected by the revolution. No one but a soulless body can live there without being stirred to the depths by it.

I reached Russia in November—the month of the Fourth Congress of the Communist International and the Fifth Anniversary of the Russian Revolution. The whole revolutionary nation was mobilized to honor the occasion, Petrograd was magnificent in red flags and streamers. Red flags fluttered against the snow from all the great granite buildings. Railroad trains, street cars, factories, stores, hotels, schools—all wore decorations. It was a festive month of celebration in which I, as a member of the Negro race, was a very active participant. I was received as though the people had been apprised of, and were prepared for, my coming. When Max Eastman and I tried to bore our way through the dense crowds that jammed the Tverskaya Street in Moscow on the seventh of November, I was caught, tossed up into the air, and passed along by dozens of stalwart youths.

"How warmly excited they get over a strange face!" said Eastman. A young Russian Communist remarked: "But where is the difference. Some of the Indians are as dark as you." To which another replied: "The lines of the face are different, the Indians have been with us long. The people instinctively see the difference." And so always the conversation revolved around me until my face flamed. The Moscow press printed long articles about the Negroes in America, a poet was inspired to rhyme about the Africans looking to Soviet Russia and soon I was in demand everywhere—at lectures of poets and journalists, the meetings of soldiers and factory workers. Slowly I began losing self-consciousness with the realization that I was welcomed thus as a symbol, as a member of the great American Negro group—kin to the unhappy Black slaves of European imperialism in Africa—that the workers of Soviet Russia, rejoicing in their freedom, were greeting through me.

Chapter Four

The Emergence of Black Power

The Black Power Movement is a conscious attempt to harness the emotional power of Black Nationalism to a practical program for the elimination of racial oppression in America. The strength shared by all American Black Nationalist movements has been their ability to engage the pride and imagination of the Black community, in ways that integrationist leaders and programs cannot. For a Negro to seek integration into American society means to identify with the values of a society that has oppressed and degraded him, to repress his natural hostility against a people who have mistreated him and to seek their approval and acceptance by continually proving his worth. The Black Nationalist, venting his hatred and freely accepting his own identity has obvious psychological advantages.

"I would laugh at my running partner, George, when he would pile layers of bleach cream on his face," writes Claude Brown, describing his experience with the assimilationist-minded sons and daughters of "the unwillingly Black middle class" at Howard University.* "I'd ask, 'What are you doin', baby, trying to get White?' His poking reply was always, 'Man, they ain't electing

---

* Claude Brown wrote the famous *Manchild in the Promised Land*, which vividly describes life in the Harlem ghetto.

no Black cats President this year.' " Brown also wrote of the changes that came with the resurgence of Black Nationalism in the 1950's.

> There was an inflaming young actor orator and political activist on the rampage. Malcolm X was light-brown skinned and screaming that he was black, black, black and would rather die than be otherwise. Black people throughout the country became afflicted with his pride.*

Black Nationalist movements have, however, historically been unable to direct the emotional commitments of their followers in functional directions. William Worthy, a prominent modern radical, points to that problem in analyzing the shortcomings of the Black Muslims, who drew wide attention in the 1950's by their successes in organizing among the poorest and most degraded elements of the Negro population.

> Their off-and-on propounding of a "separate state" and at other times, their equally unrealistic calls for a Back-to-Africa Movement have cost them the intellectual respect of many who never actually joined the all-Black sect but nevertheless admired the leaders' militancy, their forthright analysis of the forces behind the Negro's exploitation, and their triumphant self-emancipation from America's vast indoctrination apparatus. . . . The universal complaint today is that the Muslims are all talk and no action.†

The most powerful critique of the Black Nationalist tradition has always been that it provided no realistic hope for the material advancement of the race. The opponents of Black Zionism argued persuasively that the emigration of any significant portion of the free Negro population would strengthen, rather than weaken slavery and racism by eliminating their foremost opponents. Marcus Garvey's enemies made the same telling point in the 1920's. Bayard Rustin, the most articulate critic of Black Power, presents a strong case for his view that "coalition politics," the formation of political alliances with White interest groups pursuing similar economic and political goals, holds out greater hope for the rapid material amelioration of the Black man's lot in America.

> . . . Negroes, despite exhortations from SNCC . . . are going to stay in the Democratic party—to them it is the party of progress, the New Deal, the New Frontier, and the Great Society—and they are right to stay. For SNCC's Black Panther perspective is simultaneously utopian and reaction—the former for the by now obvious reason that one-tenth of the

---

* Claude Brown, "Nobody Worries About Integration Anymore," *Look* (June 27, 1967), 28.

† William Worthy, "Implications of an American Insurrection," *The Realist*, No. 62 (September, 1966), 18.

population cannot accomplish much by itself, the latter because of political struggle in this country, . . . and would give priority to the issue of race precisely at a time when the fundamental questions facing the Negro and American society alike are economic and social.*

But the more sophisticated adherents of Black Power have recognized and responded to this problem. Their reply is that the techniques of coalition politics have never achieved any lasting success because its practitioners have not succeeded in uniting and galvanizing the Black masses. Black Power, they argue, is potentially able to do so.

The concept of Black Power rests on a fundamental premise: *Before a group can enter the open society, it must first close ranks.* By this we mean that group solidarity is necessary before a group can operate effectively from a bargaining position of strength in a pluralistic society.†

What Black Power hopes to accomplish is to preserve the organizational appeal of traditional Black Nationalism, purged of the mysticism and uptopianism that has characterized it in the past, and make it an effective instrument of social change. The documents in this chapter present some of the influences that have shaped the ideal of Black Power, together with assessments of the movement and its prospects.

Every Freedom Movement Is Labeled Communist (1962)**

Robert F. Williams

Robert F. Williams as president of the NAACP chapter of Monroe, North Carolina, told his followers to arm themselves for self-defense and for retaliation against attacks by White racists. The adverse publicity given his statements and activities led to an attempt to suspend him by the National Office of the NAACP in 1959. Williams continued his activities. In 1961 he was ac-

---

* Bayard Rustin, " 'Black Power' and Coalition Politics," *Commentary* (September, 1966), 35–36.

† Stokely Carmichael and Charles V. Hamilton, *Black Power: The Politics of Liberation in America* (New York: Vintage Books, 1967), p. 44.

** Robert F. Williams, *Negroes With Guns* (New York: 1962), pp. 117–124, copyright, Marzani and Munzell, Inc., 1962. Used by permission of Marzani and Munzell.

cused of kidnapping on the basis of an incident that occurred in the course of a series of civil-rights demonstrations. He then fled to Cuba. He has since lived in exile in socialist countries from which he writes and broadcasts news bulletins with a strong nationalist and Marxist flavor into the United States.

I'm not a member and I've never been a member of the Communist Party. But most decent-minded Americans should realize by now that every movement for freedom that is initiated in the United States; every movement for human dignity, for decency; every movement that seeks fairness and social justice; every movement for human rights, is branded as "Communistic." Whenever a White person participates in a movement for Black liberation, the movement is automatically branded as "under the domination of Moscow." I can't expect to be an exception.

This Communist-thing is becoming an old standard. An old standard accusation now. Anyone who uncompromisingly opposes the racists, anyone who scorns the religious fanatics and the super-duper American conservatives is considered a Communist.

This sort of thing gives the Communists a lot of credit, because certainly many people in my movement in the South don't know what a Communist is. Most of our people have never even heard of Marx. When you say "Marx," some of the people would think that maybe you were talking about a fountain pen or a New York City cab driver. Or the movie comedians.

But people aspire to be free. People want to be liberated when they are oppressed. No matter where the leadership comes from. The enslavement and suppression of Negroes in the American South were going on before Karl Marx was born, and Negroes have been rebelling against their oppression before Marxism came into existence. As far back as the sixteenth century, and the beginning of the seventeenth century, Negroes were even rebelling on the slave ships. The history of American Negro slavery was marked by very many conspiracies and revolts on the part of Negroes.

Certainly the Marxists have participated in the human-rights struggle of Negroes, but Negroes need not be told by any philosophy or by any political party that racial oppression is wrong. Racial oppression itself inspires the Negro to rebellion. And it is on this ground that the people of Monroe refused to conform to the standard of Jim Crow life in a Jim Crow society. It is on this basis that they have struck out against the insanity of racial prejudice. We know that the southern bigot, the southern racist is mentally ill; that he is sick. The fact that Jim Crow discrimination and racial segregation may very well be based on economic exploitation is beside the point.

We are oppressed and no matter what the original cause or purpose of this oppression, the mind and personality of the racist doing the oppressing have been warped for so long that he is a mental case. Even if the economic situation is changed it will take quite a while, and it will require quite a shock, to cure this mental disease. I've read that one of the best treatments for some forms of mental illness is the shock treatment. And the shock treatment must come primarily from the Afro-American people themselves in conjunction with their White allies; in conjunction with the White youth.

This movement that I led was not a political organization. It had no political affiliations whatsoever. It was a movement of people who resented oppression. But I would say one thing about our movement. What happened in Monroe, North Carolina, had better become a lesson to the oppressors and the racists of America. Because it is symbolic of a new attitude, symbolic of a new era. It means that there will be many more racial explosions in the days to come. Monroe was just the beginning. I dare predict that Monroe will become the symbol of the new Afro-American; a symbol of the Afro-American determined to rid himself of the stigma of race prejudice and the pain and torture of race hate and oppression at any cost.

The label "Black Nationalist" is as meaningless as the Communist label. The Afro-American resents being set aside and oppressed, resents not being allowed to enter the mainstream of American society. These people who form their own groups, because they have been rejected, and start trying to create favorable societies of their own are called Black Nationalists.

This is a misleading title. Because the first thing you must remember is that I am an Afro-American and *I've* been denied the right to enter the mainstream of society in the United States. As an Afro-American I am rejected and discriminated against. We are the most excluded, the most discriminated-against group in the United States; the most discriminated-against class. So it is only normal that I direct most of my energy toward the liberation of my people, who are the most oppressed class.

As for being a Black Nationalist, this is a word that's hard to define. No, I'm not a Black Nationalist to the point that I would exclude Whites or that I would discriminate against Whites or that I would be prejudiced toward Whites. I would prefer to think of myself as an "Inter-Nationalist." That is, I'm interested in the problems of all mankind. I'm interested in the problems of Africa, of Asia, and of Latin America. I believe that we all have the same struggle; a struggle for liberation. Discrimination and race hatred are undesirable, and I'm just as much against racial discrimination, in all forms, every place in the world, as I am against it in the United States.

What do you mean by "nationalism"? When you consider the present White American society it can be classified as nothing but a nationalistic society based on race. Yet as soon as an Afro-American speaks out for his people, and is conscious and proud of his people's historical roots and culture, he becomes a "nationalist." I don't mind these labels. I don't care what they call me. I believe in justice for all people. And because the Afro-American is the most exploited, the most oppressed in our society, I believe in working foremost for his liberation.

The tactics of nonviolence will continue and should continue. We too believed in nonviolent tactics in Monroe. We've used these tactics; we've used all tactics. But we also believe that any struggle for liberation should be a flexible struggle. We shouldn't take the attitude that one method alone is the way to liberation. This is to become dogmatic. This is to fall into the same sort of dogmatism practiced by some of the religious fanatics. We can't afford to develop this type of attitude.

We must use nonviolence as a means as long as this is feasible, but the day will come when conditions become so pronounced that nonviolence will be suicidal in itself. The day is surely coming when we will see more violence on the same American scene. The day is surely coming when some of the same Negroes who have denounced our using weapons for self-defense will be arming themselves. There are those who pretend to be horrified by the idea that a Black veteran who shouldered arms for the United States would willingly take up weapons to defend his wife, his children, his home, and his life. These same people will one day be the loud advocates of self-defense. When violent racism and fascism strike at their families and their homes, not in a token way but in an all-out bloody campaign, then they will be among the first to advocate self-defense. They will justify their position as a question of survival. When it is no longer some distant Negro who's no more than a statistic, no more than an article in a newspaper; when it is no longer their neighbors, but it means them and it becomes a matter of personal salvation, then will their attitude change.

As a tactic, we use and approve nonviolent resistance. But we also believe that a man cannot have human dignity if he allows himself to be abused. to be kicked and beaten to the ground, to allow his wife and children to be attacked, refusing to defend himself on the basis that he's so pious, so self-righteous, that it would demean his personality if he fought back.

We know that the average Afro-American is not a pacifist. He's not a pacifist and he has never been a pacifist and he's not made of the type of material that would make a good pacifist. Those who doubt that the great majority of Negroes are not pacifists, just let them slap one. Pick up any Negro on any street corner in the U.S.A. and they'll find out how much he believes in turning the other cheek.

All those who dare to attack are going to learn the hard way that the Afro-American is not a pacifist. that he cannot forever be counted on not to defend himself. Those who attack him brutally and ruthlessly can no longer expect to attack him with impunity.

The Afro-American cannot forget that his enslavement in this country did not pass because of pacifist moral force or noble appeals to the Christian conscience of the slaveholders.

Henry David Thoreau is idealized as an apostle of nonviolence, the writer who influenced Gandhi, and through Gandhi, Martin Luther King, Jr. But Thoreau was not dogmatic. his eyes were open and he saw clearly. I keep with me a copy of Thoreau's *Plea For Captain John Brown*. There are truths that are just as evident in 1962 as they were in 1859 when he wrote:

> . . . It was his [John Brown's] peculiar doctrine that a man has a perfect right to interfere by force with the slaveholder, in order to rescue the slave. I agree with him. They who are continually shocked by slavery have some right to be shocked by the violent death of the slaveholder, but such will be more shocked by his life than by his death. I shall not be forward to think him mistaken in his method who quickest succeeds to liberate the slave.

I speak for the slave when I say, that I prefer the philanthrophy of Captain Brown to that philanthropy which neither shoots me nor liberates me. . . . I do not wish to kill nor to be killed, but I can foresee circumstances in which both these things would be by me unavoidable. We preserve the so-called peace of our community by deeds of petty violence every day. Look at the jail! . . . We are hoping only to live safely on the outskirts of this provisional army. So we defend ourselves and our henroosts, and maintain slavery. I know that the mass of my countrymen think that the only righteous use that can be made of Sharp's rifles and revolvers is to fight duels with them, when we are insulted by other nations, or to hunt Indians, or shoot fugitive slaves with them, or the like. I think that for once the Sharp's rifles and the revolvers were employed in a righteous cause. The tools were in the hands of one who could use them.

The same indignation that is said to have cleared the temple once will clear it again. The question is not about the weapon, but the spirit in which you use it. No man has appeared in America, as yet, who loved his fellowman so well, and treated him so tenderly. He [John Brown] lived for him. He took up his life and he laid it down for him. What sort of violence is that which is encouraged, not by soldiers, but by peaceable citizens, not so much by laymen as by ministers of the Gospel, not so much by the fighting sects as by the Quakers, and not so much by Quaker men as by Quaker women?

This event advertises me that there is such a fact as death; the possibility of a man's dying. It seems as if no man ever lived in America before; for in order to die you must first have lived.

It is in the nature of the American Negro, the same as all other men, to fight and try to destroy those things that block his path to a greater happiness in life.

Whenever I speak on the English-language radio station in Havana (which broadcasts for an audience in the United States) I hope in some way to penetrate the mental barriers and introduce new disturbing elements into the consciousness of White America. I hope to make them aware of the monstrous evil that they are party to by oppressing the Negro. Somehow, I must manage to clearly reflect the image of evil that is inherent in a racist society so that White America will be able to honestly and fully see themselves as they really are. To see themselves with the same clarity as foreigners see them and to recognize that they are not champions of democracy. To understand that today they do not really even *believe* in democracy. To understand that the world is changing regardless of whether they *think* they like it or not. For I know that if they had a glimpse of their own reality the shock would be of great therapeutic value. There would be many decent Americans who would then understand that this society must mend its ways if it is to survive; that there is no place in the world now for a racist nation.

As an individual, I'm not inclined toward "politics." The only thing I care about is justice and liberation. I don't belong to any political party. But I think that as long as the present politics prevails the Negro is not going to be integrated into American society. There will have to be great political changes before that can come about.

Those Americans who most deny the logic of the future are the ones who have driven me into exile. Those people have been cruel. Yet cruel as it may be, this exile was not the end those people had planned for me. But it is not in the hands of today's oppressors to determine my end. Their role in history denies to them an understanding of this, just as their role will not allow them to understand that every true nationalist leader in Africa has been imprisoned or exiled, and that the future leaders of Latin America and Asian national liberation today are experiencing imprisonment, exile, or worse.

The future belongs to today's oppressed and I shall be witness to that future in the liberation of the Afro-American.

Who Is the Real Villain — Uncle Tom or Simon Legree? (1966)*

SNCC Position Paper on Black Power

The Student Non-Violent Coordinating Committee grew out of a spontaneous student sit-in to desegregate a lunch counter in Greensboro, North

---

* *New York Times* (August 5, 1966).

Carolina in 1960. Originally designed to coordinate nonviolent civil-rights demonstrations, SNCC quickly became a cadre of dedicated and daring professional activists who carried on a form of running guerilla warfare with the racist authorities of the southern states. Pushed increasingly in radical directions by the successful resistance of the Deep South to its tactics, many SNCC members turned to socialist and Black Nationalist sources for guidance. In 1966, SNCC shocked its White liberal supporters by expelling its White members and abandoning its original integrationist ideas in favor of the doctrine of Black Power explained below.

The myth that the Negro is somehow incapable of liberating himself, is lazy, etc., came out of the American experience. In the books that children read, Whites are always "good" (good symbols are white), Blacks are "evil" or seen as savages in movies, their language is referred to as a "dialect," and Black people in this country are supposedly descended from savages.

Any White person who comes into the movement has these concepts in his mind about Black people if only subconsciously. He cannot escape them because the whole society has geared his subconscious in that direction.

Miss America coming from Mississippi has a chance to represent all of America, but a Black person from either Mississippi or New York will never represent America. So that White people coming into the movement cannot relate to the Black experience, cannot relate to the word "black," cannot relate to chitterlings, hog's head cheese, pig feet, ham hocks, and cannot relate to slavery, because these things are not a part of their experience. They also cannot relate to the Black religious experience, nor to the Black church unless, of course, this church has taken on White manifestations.

Negroes in this country have never been allowed to organize themselves because of White interference. As a result of this, the stereotype has been reinforced that Blacks cannot organize themselves. The White psychology that Blacks have to be watched, also reinforces this stereotype. Blacks, in fact, feel intimidated by the presence of Whites, because of their knowledge of the power that Whites have over their lives. One White person can come into a meeting of Black people and change the complexion of that meeting, whereas one Black person would not change the complexion of that meeting unless he was an obvious Uncle Tom. People would immediately start talking about "brotherhood," "love," etc.; race would not be discussed.

If people must express themselves freely, there has to be a climate in which they can do this. If Blacks feel intimidated by Whites, then they are not liable to vent the rage that they feel about Whites in the presence of Whites—specially not the Black people whom we are trying to organize, i.e., the broad masses of Black people. A climate has to be created whereby Blacks can express themselves. The reason that Whites must be excluded is not that one is anti-White, but because the efforts that one is trying to achieve cannot succeed because Whites have intimidating effect. Offtimes the intimidating effect is in direct proportion to the amount of degradation that Black people have suffered at the hands of White people.

It must be offered that White people who desire change in this country should go where that problem (of racism) is most manifest. The problem is not in the Black community. The White people should go into White communities where the Whites have created power for the express (purpose) of denying Blacks dignity and self-determination. Whites who come into the Black community with ideas of change seem to want to absolve the power structure of its responsibility of what it is doing and saying that change can come only through Black unity, which is only the worst kind of parentalism. This is not to say that Whites have not had an importance in the movement. In the case of Mississippi, their role was very key in that they helped give Blacks the right to organize, but that role is now over, and it should be.

People now have the right to picket, the right to give leaflets, the right to vote, the right to demonstrate, the right to print.

These things which revolve around the right to organize have been accomplished mainly because of the entrance of White people into Mississippi, in the summer of 1946. Since these goals have now been accomplished, their [the Whites'] role in the movement has now ended. What does it mean if Black people, once having the right to organize, are not allowed to organize themselves? It means that Blacks' ideals about inferiority are being reinforced. Shouldn't people be able to organize themselves? Blacks should be given this right. Further [White] participation means in the eyes of the Black community that Whites are the "brains" behind the movement and

Blacks cannot function without Whites. This only serves to perpetuate existing attitudes within the existing society, i.e., Blacks
are "dumb," "unable to take care of business," etc. Whites are
"smart," the "brains" behind everything.

How do Blacks relate to other Blacks as such? How do we react
to Willie Mays as against Mickey Mantle? What is our response
to Mays hitting a home run against Mantle performing the same
deed? One has to come to the conclusion that it is because of Black
participation in baseball. Negroes still identify with the Dodgers
because of Jackie Robinson's efforts with the Dodgers. Negroes
would instantly champion all-Black teams if they opposed all-White
or predominantly White teams. The same principle operates for the
movement as it does for baseball: a mystique must be created
whereby Negroes can identify with the movement.

Thus an all-Black project is needed in order for the people to
free themselves. This has to exist from the beginning. This relates
to what can be called "coalition politics." There is no doubt in our
minds that some Whites are just as disgusted with this system as
we are. But it is meaningless to talk about coalition if there is no
one to align yourself with, because of the lack of organization in
the White communities. There can be no talk of "hooking up" unless
Black people organize Blacks and White people organize Whites.
If these conditions are met then perhaps at some later date—and
if we are going in the same direction—talks about exchange of
personnel, coalition, and other meaningful alliances can be discussed.

In the beginning of the movement, we had fallen into a trap
whereby we thought that our problems revolved around the right
to eat in certain lunch counters or the right to vote or to organize
our communities. We have seen, however, that the problem is much
deeper. The problem of this country, as we had seen it, concerned
all Blacks and all Whites. [Therefore] if decisions were left to the
young people, then solutions would be arrived at. But this negates
the history of Black people and Whites. We have dealt stringently
with the problem of "Uncle Tom," but we have not yet gotten
around to Simon Legree. We must ask ourselves who is the real
villain? Uncle Tom or Simon Legree? Everyone knows Uncle Tom
but who knows Simon Legree?

So what we have now [in SNCC] is a closed society. A clique.
Black people cannot relate to SNCC, because of its unrealistic non-

racial atmosphere; denying their experience of America as a racist society. In contrast, SCLC [the Reverend Dr. Martin Luther King, Jr.'s Southern Christian Leadership Conference] has a staff that at least maintains a Black facade. The front office is virtually all Black, but nobody accuses SCLC of being racist.

If we are to proceed toward true liberation, we must cut ourselves off from White people. We must form our own institutions, credit unions, co-ops, political parties, write our own histories.

To proceed further, let us make some comparisons between the Black Movement of the [early] 1900's and the movement of the 1960's—the NAACP [the National Association for the Advancement of Colored People] with SNCC. Whites subverted the Niagra movement [the forerunner of the NAACP] which, at the outset, was an all-Black movement. The name of the new organization was also very revealing, in that it presupposed Blacks had to be advanced to the level of Whites. We are now aware that the NAACP has grown reactionary, is controlled by the Black power structure itself and stands as one of the main roadblocks to Black freedom. SNCC, by allowing Whites to remain in the organization, can have its efforts subverted in the same manner, i.e., by having them play important roles such as community organizers, etc. Indigenous leadership cannot be built with Whites in the positions they now hold.

These facts do not mean that Whites cannot help. They can participate on a voluntary basis. We can contract work out to them, but in no way can they participate on a policy-making level.

The charge may be made that we are "racists," but Whites who are sensitive to our problems will realize that we must determine our own destiny.

In an attempt to find a solution to our dilemma, we propose that our organization [SNCC] should be Black-staffed, Black-controlled and black-financed. We do not want to fall into a similar dilemma that other civil-rights organizations have fallen. If we continue to rely on White financial support we will find ourselves entwined in the tentacles of the White power complex that controls this country. It is also important that a Black organization (devoid of cultism) be projected to our people so that it can be demonstrated that such organizations are viable.

More and more we see Black people in this country being used as a tool of the White liberal establishment. Liberal Whites have not begun to address themselves to the real problem of Black people in this country; witness their bewilderment, fear and anxiety when nationalism is mentioned concerning Black people. An analysis of their [White liberals'] reaction to the word alone [*nationalism*] reveals a very meaningful attitude of Whites of any ideological persuasion toward Blacks in this country. It means previous solutions to Black problems in this country have been made in the interests of those Whites dealing with these problems and not in the best interests of Black people in this country. Whites can only subvert our true search and struggle for self-determination, self-identification, and liberation in this country. Re-evaluation of the White and Black roles must *now* take place so that Whites no longer designate roles that Black people play but rather Black people define White people's roles.

Too long have we allowed White people to interpret the importance and meaning of the cultural aspects of our society. We have allowed them to tell us what was good about our Afro-American music, art and literature. How many Black critics do we have on the "jazz" scene? How can a White person who is not part of the Black psyche (except in the oppressor's role) interpret the meaning of the blues to us who are manifestations of the songs themselves, It must also be pointed out that on whatever level of contact that Blacks and Whites come together, that meeting or confrontation is not on the level of the Blacks but always on the level of the Whites. This only means that our everyday contact with Whites is a reinforcement of the myth of White supremacy. Whites are the ones who must try to raise themselves to our humanistic level. We are not, after all, the ones who are responsible for a genocidal war in Vietnam; we are not responsible for neocolonialism in Africa and Latin America; we are not the ones who held a people in animalistic bondage over 400 years. We reject the American dream as defined by White people and must work to construct an American reality defined by Afro-Americans.

One of the criticisms of White militants and radicals is that when we view the masses of White people we view the overall reality of America, we view the racism, the bigotry, and the distortion of personality, we view man's inhumanity to man; we view in reality 180 million racists. The sensitive White intellectual and radical who is fighting to bring about change is conscious of this fact, but does not have the courage to admit this. When he admits this reality, then he must also admit his own involvement because he is a part of the collective White America. It is only to the extent that he recognizes this that he will be able to change this reality.

Another concern is how does the White radical view the Black community and how does he view the poor White community in terms of organizing. So far, we have found that most White radicals have sought to escape the horrible reality of America by going into the Black community and attempting to organize Black people while neglecting the organization of their own people's racist communities.How can one clean up someone else's yard when one's own yard is untidy? Again we feel that SNCC and the Civil Rights Movement in general is in many aspects similar to the anticolonial situations in the African and Asian countries. We have the Whites in the movement corresponding to the White civil servants and missionaries in the colonial countries who have worked with the colonial people for a long period of time and have developed a parentalistic attitude toward them. The reality of the colonial people taking over their own lives and controlling their own destiny must be faced. Having to move aside and letting this natural process of growth and development take place must be faced.

These views should not be equated with outside influence or outside agitation but should be viewed as the natural process of growth and development within a movement; so that the move by the Black militants and SNCC in this direction should be viewed as a turn toward self-determination.

It is very ironic and curious how aware Whites in this country can champion anticolonialism in other countries, in Africa, Asia, and Latin America, but when Black people move toward similar goals of self-determination in this country they are viewed as racists and anti-White by these same progressive Whites. In proceeding further, it can be said that this attitude derives from the overall point of view of the White psyche as it concerns the Black people. This attitude stems from the era of the slave revolts when every White man was a potential deputy or sheriff or guardian of the state. Because when Black people got together among themselves to work out their problems, it became a threat to White people, because such meetings were potential slave revolts.

It can be maintained that this attitude or way of thinking has perpetuated itself to this current period and that it is part of the psyche of White people in this country whatever their potential persuasion might be. It is part of the White fear–guilt complex resulting from the slave revolts. There have been examples of Whites who stated that they can deal with Black fellows on an individual basis but become threatened or menaced by the presence of groups of Blacks. It can be maintained that this attitude is held by the majority of progressive Whites in this country.

A thorough re-examination must be made by Black people concerning the contributions that we have made in shaping this country. If this re-examination and re-evaluation is not made, and Black people are not given their proper due and respect, then the antagonism and contradictions are going to become more and more glaring, more and more intense until a national explosion may result.

When people attempt to move from these conclusions it would be faulty reasoning to say they are ordered by racism, because, in this country and in the West, racism has functioned as a type of White nationalism when dealing with Black people. We all know the habit that this has created throughout the world and particularly among non-White people in this country.

Therefore any re-evaluation that we must make will, for the most part, deal with identification. Who are the Black people, what are the Black people; what is their relation to America and the world?

It must be repeated that the White myth of "Negro citizenship," perpetuated by the White elite, has confused the thinking of radical and progressive Blacks and Whites in this country. The broad masses of Black people react to American society in the same manner as colonial peoples react to the West in Africa, and Latin America, and have the same relationship—that of the colonized toward the colonizer.

A Letter to Americans (1968)*

James Baldwin

James Baldwin, the noted novelist and essayist here expresses his personal reaction to Black Power. Baldwin has long been concerned with the themes of Black Nationalism. His widely read essay, "The Fire Next Time," first awakened many Americans to its potential power.

Stokely Carmichael, the young head of the Student Non-Violent Coordinating Committee who first publicized the concept of Black Power, joined the Civil Rights movement while a student at Howard University in the early 1960's. He won a reputation as one of the most spirited and daring members of SNCC during its early campaigns. Like other SNCC workers, his ideas were increasingly radicalized by the bitter resistance their efforts met with in the Deep South. By 1966 Carmichael had been jailed at least twenty-seven times for his civil-rights activities and stated that he had attended the funerals of seventeen of his co-workers. He was elected chairman of SNCC in 1966 and played a major role in developing its Black Power platform. In 1968, Carmichael left SNCC in order to affiliate with the Black Panthers, a group which, by then, he found more congenial.

I first met Stokely Carmichael in the Deep South, where he was just another nonviolent kid, marching and talking and getting his head whipped. This time now seems as far behind us as the Flood, and if those suffering, gallant, betrayed boys and girls who were then using their bodies in an attempt to save a heedless nation have since concluded that the nation is not worth saving, no American has the right to be surprised—to put the matter as mildly as it can possibly be put. Actually, Americans are not at all surprised; they exhibit all the vindictiveness of the guilty; what happened to those boys and girls, and what happened to the Civil Rights Movement, is an indictment of America and Americans, and an enduring monument which we will not outlive, to the breathtaking cowardice of this sovereign people.

Naturally, the current in which we all were struggling threw Stokely and me together from time to time—it threw many people together, including, finally, Martin Luther King and Malcolm X.

* James Baldwin, "A Letter to Americans," *Freedomways*, VIII (Spring, 1968, Second Quarter), 112–116. Copyright by Freedomways Associates, Inc., New York, 1968; used by permission of Freedomways Associates.

America sometimes resembles, at least from the point of view of the Black man, an exceedingly monotonous minstrel show; the same dances, same music, same jokes. One has done (or been) the show so long that one can do it in one's sleep. So it was not in the least surprising for me to encounter (one more time) the American surprise when Stokely—as Americans allow themselves the luxury of supposing—coined the phrase "Black Power." He didn't coin it. He simply dug it up again from where it's been lying since the first slaves hit the gangplank. I have never known a Negro in all my life who was not obsessed with Black Power.

Those representatives of White power, who are not too hopelessly brainwashed or eviscerated, will understand that the only way for a Black man in America *not* to be obsessed with the problem of how to control his destiny and protect his house, his women and his children, is for that Black man to become, in his own mind, the something less than a man which this Republic, alas, has always considered him to be. And when a Black man, whose destiny and identity have always been controlled by others, decides and states that he will control his own destiny and rejects the identity given to him by others, he is talking revolution. In point of sober fact, he cannot possibly be talking anything else, and nothing is more revelatory of the American hypocrisy than their swift perception of this fact. The "White backlash" is meaningless twentieth-century jargon designed at once to hide and to justify the fact that most White Americans are still unable to believe that the Black man is a man in the same way that we speak of the "credibility gap" because we are too cowardly to face the fact that our leaders have been lying to us for years. Perhaps we suspect that we deserve the contempt with which we allow ourselves to be treated.

In any case, I had been hoping to see Stokely again in Paris. But I now learn that he has arrived in New York and that his passport has been lifted. He is being punished by a righteous government, in the name of a justly wrathful people, and there appears to be a very strong feeling that this punishment is insufficient. If only, I gather, we had had the foresight to declare ourselves at war, we would now be able to shoot Mr. Carmichael for treason. On the other hand, even if the government's honorable hands are tied, the mob has gotten the message. I remember standing on a street corner in Selma during a voting registration drive. The Blacks lined up before the court house, under the American flag; the sheriff and his man, with their helmets and guns and clubs and cattle prods; a mob of idle White men standing on the corner. The sheriff raised his club and he and his deputies beat two Black boys to the ground. Never will I forget the surge in the mob: authority had given them their signal. The sheriff had given them the right, indeed had very nearly imposed on them the duty, to bomb and murder: and no one has ever accused that sheriff of "inciting to riot," much less of sedition. No one has ever accused ex-Governor Wallace of Alabama—"*ex*" in name only—of insurrection, although he had the Confederate flag flying from the dome of the capitol the day we marched on Montgomery. The government would like to be able to indict Stokely and many others like him of incitement to riot; but I accuse the *government* of this crime. It is, briefly, an insult to my intelligence, and to the intelligence of any Black person, to ask me to believe that the most powerful nation in the world is unable to do anything to make the lives of its Black citizens less appalling. It is not unable to do it, it is only unwilling to do it. Americans are deluded if they suppose Stokely to be the first Black man to say, "The United States is going to fall. I only hope I live to see the day." Every Black man in this howling North American wilderness has said it, and is saying it, in many, many ways, over and over again. One's only got to listen, again, to all those happy songs. Or walk to Harlem and talk to any junkie, or anybody else—if, of course, they will talk to you. It was a nonviolent Black student who told Bobby Kennedy a few years ago that he didn't know how much longer he could remain nonviolent; didn't know how much longer he could take the beatings, the bombings, the terror. He said that he would never take up arms in defense of America—never, never, never. If he ever picked up a gun, it would be for very different reasons: trembling, he shook his finger in Bobby Kennedy's face, and said, with terrible tears in his voice, "When I pull the trigger, kiss it good-bye!"

That boy has grown up, as have so many like him—we will not mention those irreparably ruined, or dead—and I really wonder what White Americans expected to happen. Did they really suppose that fifteen-year-old Black boy remained fifteen forever? Did they really suppose that the tremendous energy and the incredible courage which went into those sit-ins, wade-ins, swim-ins, picket lines, marches, was incapable of transforming itself into an overt attack on the status quo? I remember that same day in Selma watching the line of Black would-be voters walk away from the court house which they had not been allowed to enter. And I thought, the day is coming when they will not line up any more.

That day may very well be here—I fear it is here; certainly Stokely is here, and he is not alone. It helps our situation not at all to attempt to punish the man for telling the truth. I repeat: we have seen this show before. This victimization has occurred over and over again, from Frederick Douglass to Paul Robeson to Muhammad Ali to Malcolm X. And I contest the government's right to lift the passports of these people who hold views of which the government—and especially *this* government—disapproves. The government has [a] duty to warn me of the dangers I may encounter if I travel to hostile territory, though they never said anything about the probable results of my leaving Harlem to go downtown and never said anything about my travels to Alabama, but it does not have the right to use my passport as a political weapon against me, as means of bringing me to heel. These are terror tactics. Furthermore, *all* Black Americans are born into a society which is determined—repeat: determined—that they shall never learn the truth about themselves or their society, which is determined that Black men shall use as their only frame of reference that White Americans convey to them of their own potentialities, and of the shape, size, dimensions and possibilities of the world. And I do not hesitate for an instant to condemn this as a crime. To persuade Black boys and girls, as we have for so many generations, that their lives are worth less than other lives, and that they can only live on terms dictated to them by other people, by people who despise them, is worse than a crime, it is the sin against the Holy Ghost.

Now, I may not always agree with Stokely's views, or the ways in which he expresses them. My agreement, or disagreement, is absolutely irrelevant. I get his message. Stokely Carmichael, a Black man under thirty, is saying to me, a Black man over forty, that he will not live the life I've lived, or be corralled into some of the awful choices I have been forced to make. *And* he is *perfectly right*. The government and the people who have made his life, and mine, and the lives of all our forefathers, and the lives of all our brothers and sisters and women and children an indescribable hell have no right, now, to penalize the Black man, this so despised stranger here for so long, for attempting to discover if the world is as small as the Americans have told him it is. And the political implications involve nothing more and nothing less than what the Western world takes to be its material self-interest. I need scarcely state to what extent the Western self-interest and the Black self-interest find themselves at war, but it is precisely this message which the Western nations, and this one above all, will have to accept, if they expect to survive. Nothing is more unlikely than that the Western nations, and this one above all, will be able to welcome so vital a metamorphosis. We have constructed a history which is a total lie, and have persuaded ourselves that it is true. I seriously doubt that anything worse can happen to any people. One doesn't need a Stokely gloating in Havana about the hoped-for fall of the United States, and to attempt to punish him for saying what so many millions of people feel, is simply to bring closer, and make yet more deadly, the terrible day. One should listen to what's being said, and reflect on it: for many, many millions of people long for our downfall, and it is not because they are Communists. It is because ignorance is in the saddle here, and it rides mankind. Let us attempt to face the fact that we *are* a racist society, racist to the very marrow, and we are fighting a racist war. No Black man in chains in his own country, and watching the many deaths occurring around him every day, believes for a moment that America cares anything at all about the freedom of Asia. My own condition, as a Black man in America, tells me what Americans really feel and really want, and tells me who they really are. And therefore, every bombed village is my home town.

That, in a way, is what Stokely is saying, and that's why this youth can so terrify a nation. He's saying the bill is in, the party's over, are we going to live here like men or not? Bombs won't pay this bill, and bombs won't wipe it out. And Stokely did not begin his career with dreams of terror, but with dreams of love. Now he's saying, and he's not alone, and he's not the first, if I can't live here, well, then, neither will you. You couldn't have built it without me; this land is also mine; we'll share it, or we'll perish, *and I don't care!*

I *do* care—about Stokely's life, my country's life. One's seen too much already of gratuitous destruction, one hopes, always, that something will happen in the human heart which will change our common history. But if it doesn't happen, this something, if this country cannot hear and cannot change, then we, the Blacks, the most despised children of the great Western house, are simply forced, with both pride and despair, to remember that we come from a long line of runaway slaves who managed to survive without passports.

An Advocate of Black Power Defines It (1968)*

Charles V. Hamilton

Charles V. Hamilton, chairman of the Political Science Department at Roosevelt University, has written several books and articles on race and politics. His most recent work, written with Stokely Carmichael, is *Black Power: The Politics of Liberation in America.*

Black Power has many definitions and connotations in the rhetoric of race relations today. To some people, it is synonymous with premeditated acts of violence to destroy the political and economic institutions of this country. Others equate Black Power with plans to rid the Civil Rights Movement of Whites who have been in it for years. The concept is understood by many to mean hatred of and separation from Whites; it is associated with calling Whites "honkey" and with shouts of "Burn, baby, burn!" Some understand it to be the use of pressure-group tactics in the accepted tradition of the American political process. And still others say that Black Power must be seen first of all as an attempt to instill a sense of identity and pride in Black people.

Ultimately, I suspect, we have to accept the fact that in this highly charged atmosphere it is virtually impossible to come up with a single definition satisfactory to all.

Even as some of us try to articulate our idea of Black Power and the way we relate to it and advocate it, we are categorized as

---

* From Charles V. Hamilton, "An Advocate of Black Power Defines It," *The New York Times Magazine* (April 14, 1968), 22, 23, 79–83. Copyright 1968 by The New York Times Company. Reprinted by permission.

"moderate" or "militant" or "reasonable" or "extremist." "I can accept your definition of Black Power," a listener will say to me. "But how does your position compare with what Stokely Carmichael said in Cuba or with what Rap Brown said in Cambridge, Maryland?" Or, just as frequently, some young White New Left advocate will come up to me and proudly announce: "You're not radical enough. Watts, Newark, Detroit—that's what's happening, man! You're nothing but a reformist. We've got to blow up this society. Read Che or Debray or Mao." All I can do is shrug and conclude that some people believe that making a revolution in this country involves rhetoric, Molotov cocktails and being under thirty.

To have Black Power equated with calculated acts of violence would be very unfortunate. First, if Black people have learned anything over the years, it is that he who shouts revolution the loudest is one of the first to run when the action starts. Second, open calls to violence are a sure way to have one's ranks immediately infiltrated. Third—and this is as important as any reason—violent revolution in this country would fail; it would be met with the kind of repression used in Sharpeville, South Africa, in 1960, when sixty-seven Africans were killed and 186 wounded during a demonstration against apartheid. It is clear that America is not above this. There are many White bigots who would like nothing better than to embark on a program for Black genocide, even though the imposition of such repressive measures would destroy civil liberties for Whites as well as for Blacks. Some Whites are so panicky, irrational, and filled with racial hatred that they would welcome the opportunity to annihilate the Black community. This was clearly shown in the senseless murder of Dr. Martin Luther King, Jr., which understandably—but nonetheless irrationally—prompted some black militants to advocate violent retaliation. Such cries for revenge itensify racial fear and animosity when the need—now more than ever—is to establish solid, stable organizations and action programs.

Many Whites will take comfort in these words of caution against violence. But they should not. The truth is that the Black ghettoes are going to continue to blow up out of sheer frustration and rage, and no amount of rhetoric from professors writing articles in magazines (which most Black people in the ghettoes do not read anyway) will affect that. There comes a point beyond which people cannot be expected to endure prejudice, oppression, and deprivation, and they *will* explode.

Some of us can protect our positions by calling for "law and order" during a riot, or by urging "peaceful" approaches, but we should not be confident that we are being listened to by Black people legitimately fed up with intolerable conditions. If White America wants a solution to the violence in the ghettos by Blacks, then let White America end the violence done to the ghettoes by Whites. We simply must come to understand that there can be no social order without social justice. "How long will the violence in the summers last?" another listener may ask. "How intransigent is White America?" is my answer. And the answer to that could be just more rhetoric or it could be a sincere response to legitimate demands.

Black Power must not be naive about the intentions of White decision-makers to yield anything without a struggle and a confrontation by organized power. Black people will gain only as much as they can win through their ability to organize independent bases of economic and political power—through boycotts, electoral activity, rent strikes, work stoppages, pressure-group bargaining. And it must be clear that Whites will have to bargain with Blacks or continue to fight them in the streets of the Detroits and the Newarks. Rather than being a call to violence, this is a clear recognition that the ghetto rebellions, in addition to producing the possibility of apartheid-type repression, have been functional in moving *some* Whites to see that viable solutions must be sought.

Black Power is concerned with organizing the rage of Black people and with putting new, hard questions and demands to White America. As we do this, White America's responses will be crucial to the questions of violence and viability. Black Power must (1) deal with the obviously growing alienation of black people and their distrust of the institutions of this society; (2) work to create new values and to build a new sense of community and belonging; and (3) work to establish legitimate new institutions that make participants, not recipients, out of a people traditionally excluded from the fundamentally racist processes of this country. There is nothing glamorous about this; it involves persistence and hard, tedious, day-to-day work.

Black Power rejects the lessons of slavery and segregation that caused Black people to look upon themselves with hatred and disdain. To be "integrated" it was necessary to deny one's heritage, one's own culture, to be ashamed of one's black skin, thick lips and kinky hair. In their book, *Racial Crisis in America,* two Florida State University sociologists, Lewis M. Killian and Charles M. Grigg, wrote: "At the present time, integration as a solution to the race problem demands that the Negro foreswear his identity as a Negro. But for a lasting solution, the meaning of 'American' must lose its implicit racial modifier, 'white.' "* The Black man must change his demeaning conception of himself; he must develop a sense of pride and selfrespect. Then, if integration comes, it will deal with people who are psychologically and mentally healthy, with people who have a sense of their history and of themselves as whole human beings.

In the process of creating these new values, Black Power will, its advocates hope, build a new sense of community among Black people. It will try to forge a bond in the Black community between those who have "made it" and those "on the bottom." It will bring an end to the internal backbiting and suspicious bickering, the squabbling over tactics and personalities so characteristic of the Black community. If Black Power can produce this unity, that in itself will be revolutionary, for the Black community and for the country.

Black Power recognizes that new forms of decision-making must be implemented in the Black community. One purpose, clearly, is to overcome the alienation and distrust.

Let me deal with this specifically by looking at the situation in terms of "internal" and "external" ghetto problems and approaches. When I speak of internal problems, I refer to such things as exploitative merchants who invade the Black communities, to absentee slumlords to inferior schools and arbitrary law enforcement, to Black people unable to develop their own independent economic and political bases. There are, of course, many problems facing Black people which must be dealt with outside the ghettoes: jobs, open occupancy, medical care, higher education.

---

* Lewis M. Killian and Charles M. Grigg, *Racial Crisis in America: Leadership in Conflict* (Englewood Cliffs, New Jersey: Prentice-Hall, Inc., 1964).

The solution of the internal problems does not require the presence of massive numbers of Whites marching arm-in-arm with Blacks. Local all-Black groups can organize boycotts of disreputable merchants and of those employers in the Black communities who fail to hire and promote Black people. Already, we see this approach spreading across the country with Operation Breadbasket, initiated by Dr. King's Southern Leadership Conference. The national director of the program, the Reverend Jesse Jackson, who was with Dr. King when he was murdered in Memphis, has established several such projects from Los Angeles to Raleigh, North Carolina.

In Chicago alone, in fifteen months, approximately 2,000 jobs, worth more than $15 million in annual income were obtained for Black people. Negotiations are conducted on hiring and upgrading Black people, marketing the products of Black manufacturers and suppliers, and providing contracts to Black companies. The operation relies heavily on the support of Black businessmen, who are willing to work with Operation Breadbasket because it is mutually beneficial. They derive a profit and in turn contribute to the economic development of the Black community.

This is Black Power in operation. But there is not nearly enough of this kind of work going on. In some instances, there is a lack of technical know-how coupled with a lack of adequate funds. These two defects constantly plague constructive pressure-group activity in the Black communities.

CORE (Congress of Racial Equality) has developed a number of cooperatives around the country. In Opelousas, Louisiana, it has organized over 300 Black farmers, growers of sweet potatoes, cabbages and okra, in the Grand-Marie Co-op. They sell their produce and some of the income goes back into the co-op as dues. Initially, 20 per cent of the cooperative's members were White farmers, but most of the Whites dropped out as a result of social and economic pressures from the White community. An off-shoot of the Grand-Marie group is the Southern Consumer's Cooperative in Lafayette, Louisiana, which makes and sells fruit cakes and candy. It has been in existence for more than a year, employes approximately 150 Black people and has led to the formation of several credit unions and buying clubs.

The major effort of Black Power-oriented CORE is in the direction of economic development. Antoine Perot, program director of

CORE, says: "One big need in the Black community is to develop capital-producing instruments which create jobs. Otherwise, we are stuck with the one-crop commodity—labor—which does not produce wealth. Mere jobs are not enough. These will simply perpetuate Black dependency."

Thus, small and medium-sized businesses are being developed in the Black communities of Chicago, San Francisco, Detroit, Cleveland, New York and several other urban centers. CORE hopes to call on some successful Black businessmen around the country as consultants, and it is optimistic that they will respond favorably with their know-how and, in some instances, their money. The goal is to free as many Black people as possible from economic dependency in many places that has hampered effective independent political organizing.

In New York, Black Power, in the way we see it, operates through a group called NEGRO [National Economic Growth and Reconstruction Organization]. Its acronym does not sit too well with some advocates of Black consciousness who see in the use of the term "Negro" an indication of less than sufficient pride. Started in 1964, the group deals with economic self-help for the Black community: a hospital in Queens, a chemical corporation, a textile company and a construction company. NEGRO, with an annual payroll of $1 million and assets of $3 million, is headed by Dr. Thomas W. Matthew, a neurosurgeon who has been accused of failing to file income-tax returns for 1961, 1962 and 1963. He has asserted that he will pay all the government says he owes, but not until "my patient is cured or one of us dies." His patient is the Black community, and the emphasis of his group is on aiding Blacks and reducing reliance on the White man. The organization creates a sense of identity and cohesiveness that is painfully lacking in much of the Black community.

In helping oneself and one's race through hard work, NEGRO would appear to be following the Puritan ethic of work and achievement: if you work hard, you will succeed. One gets the impression that the organization is not necessarily idealistic about this. It believes that Black people will never develop in this country as long as they must depend on handouts from the White man. This is realism, whatever ethic it is identified with. And this, too, is Black Power in operation.

More frequently than not, projects will not use the term "Black Power," but that is hardly necessary. There is, for instance, the Poor People's Corporation, formed by a former SNCC [Student Nonviolent Coordinating Committee] worker, Jesse Norris, in August, 1965. It has set up fifteen cooperatives in Mississippi, employing about 200 Black people. The employes, all shareholders, make handbags, hats, dresses, quilts, dolls and other handcraft items that are marketed through Liberty House in Jackson, Mississippi. Always sensitive to the development of the Black community, the Poor People's Corporation passed a rule that only registered voters could work in the co-ops.

These enterprises are small; they do not threaten the economic structure of this society, but their members look upon them as vital for the development of the Black people. Their purpose is to establish a modicum of economic self-sufficiency without focusing too much attention on the impact they will have on the American economic system.

Absolutely crucial to the development of Black Power is the Black middle class. These are people with sorely needed skills. There has been a lot of discussion about where the Black middle class stands in relation to Black Power. Some people adopt the view that most members of the class opt out of the race (or at least try to do so) ; they get good jobs, a nice home, two cars, and forget about the masses of Blacks who have not "made it." This has been largely true. Many middle-class Blacks simply do not feel an obligation to help the less fortunate members of their race.

There is, however, a growing awareness among Black middle-class people of their role in the Black revolution. On January 20, a small group of them (known, appropriately enough, as the Catalysts) called an all-day conference in a South Side Chicago church to discuss ways of linking Black middle-class professionals with Black people in the lower class. Present were about 370 people of all sorts: teachers, social workers, lawyers, accountants, three physicians, housewives, writers. They met in workshops to discuss ways of making their skills and positions relevant to the Black society, and they held no press conferences. Though programs of action developed, the truth is that they remain the exception, not the rule, in the Black middle class.

Another group has been formed by Black teachers in Chicago, Detroit and New York, and plans are being made to expand. In Chicago, the organization is called the Association of Afro-American Educators. These are people who have traditionally been the strongest supporters of the status quo. Education is intended to develop people who will support the existing values of the society and "Negro" teachers have been helping this process over the years. But now some of them (more than 250 met on February 12 in Chicago) are organizing and beginning to redefine, first, their role as Black educators vis-a-vis the black revolution, and, second, the issues as they see them. Their motivation is outlined in the following statement:

> By tapping our vast resources of Black intellectual expertise, we shall generate new ideas for *meaningful* educational programs, curricula and instructional materials which will contribute substantially toward raising the educational achievement of Black children.
>
> Our purpose is to extricate ourselves momentarily from the dominant society in order to realign our priorities, to mobilize and to "get ourselves together" to do what must be done by those best equipped to do it.

This is what they *say:* whether they can pull it off will depend initially on their ability to bring along their Black colleagues, many of whom, admittedly, do not see the efficacy of such an attitude. Unless the link is made between the Black middle-class professionals and the Black masses, Black Power will probably die on the speaker's platform.

Another important phenomenon in the development of Black Power is the burgeoning of Black students' groups on college campuses across the country. I have visited seventeen such campuses— from Harvard to Virginia to Wisconsin to U.C.L.A.—since October. The students are discussing problems of identity, of relevant curricula at their universities, of ways of helping their people when they graduate. Clearly, one sees in these hundreds (the figure could be in the thousands) of Black students a little bit of Booker T. Washington (self-help and the dignity of common labor) and a lot of W. E. B. Du Bois (vigorous insistence on equality and the liberal education of the most talented Black men).

These are the people who are planning to implement social, political and economic Black Power in their home towns. They will run for public office, aware that Richard Hatcher started from a political base in the Black community. He would not be Mayor of Gary, Indiana, today if he had not first mobilized the Black voters. Some people point out that he had to have White support. This is true; in many instances such support is necessary, but internal unity is necessary first.

This brings us to a consideration of the external problems of the Black community. It is clear that Black people will need the help of Whites at many places along the line. There simply are not sufficient economic resources—actual or potential—in the black community for a total, unilateral, bootstrap operation. Why should there be? Black people have been the target of deliberate denial for centuries, and racist America has done its job well. This is a serious problem that must be faced by Black Power advocates. On the one hand, they recognize the need to be independent of the "White power structure." And on the other, they must frequently turn to that structure for help—technical and financial. Thus, the rhetoric and the reality often clash.

Resolution probably lies in the realization by White Americans that it is in their interest not to have a weak, dependent, alienated Black community inhabiting the inner cities and blowing them up periodically. Society needs stability, and as long as there is a sizable powerless, restless group within it which considers the society illegitimate, stability is not possible. However it is calculated, the situation calls for a Black–White reapprochement, which may well come only through additional confrontations and crises. More frequently than not, the self-interest of the dominant society is not clearly perceived until the brink is reached.

There are many ways Whites can relate to this phenomenon. First, they must recognize that Blacks are going to insist on an equitable distribution of *decision-making power*. Anything less will simply be perpetuating a welfare mentality among blacks. And if the society thinks only in terms of *giving* more jobs, better schools and more housing, the result will be the creation of more Black recipients still dependent on Whites.

The equitable distribution of power must result from a conviction that it is a matter of mutual self-interest, not from the feelings of guilt and altruism that were evident at the National Conference of New Politics convention in Chicago in August 1967. An equitable distribution means that Black men will have to occupy positions of political power in precincts, counties, congressional districts and cities where their numbers and organization warrant. It means the end of absentee White ward committeemen and precinct captains in Chicago's Black precincts.

But this situation is much easier described than achieved. Black Americans generally are no more likely to vote independently than other Americans. In many northern urban areas, especially, the job of wooing the Black vote away from the Democratic party is gigantic. The established machine has the resources: patronage, tradition, apathy. In some instances the change will take a catalytic event—a major racial incident, a dramatic Black candidate, a serious boner by the White establishment (such as splitting the white vote). The mere call to "blackness" simply is not enough, even where the members are right.

In addition, many of the problems facing Black people can be solved only to the extent that Whites are willing to see such imperatives as an open housing market and an expanding job market. White groups must continue to bring as much pressure as possible on local and national decision-makers to adopt sound policy in these fields. These enlightened Whites *will* be able to work with Black Power groups.

There are many things which flow from this orientation to Black Power. It is not necessary that blacks create parallel agencies—political or economic—in all fields and places. In some areas, it is possible to work within, say, the two-party system. Richard Hatcher did so in Gary, but he first had to organize Black voters to fight the Democratic party machine in the primary. The same is true of Mayor Carl Stokes in Cleveland. At some point it may be wise to work within the existing agencies, but this must be done only from a base of independent, not subordinated, power.

On the other hand, dealing with a racist organization like George Wallace's Democratic party in Alabama would require forming an independent group. The same is true with some labor unions, especially in the South, which still practice discrimination despite the condemnation of such a policy by their parent unions. Many union locals are willing to work with their Black members on such matters as wages and working conditions, but refuse to join in the fight for open housing laws.

The point is that Black people must become much more pragmatic in their approach. Whether we try to work within or outside a particular agency should depend entirely on a hard-nosed, calculated examination of potential success in each situation—a careful analysis of cost and benefit. Thus, when we negotiate the test will be: How will Black people, not some political machine downtown or some labor union boss across town, benefit from this?

Black Power must insist that the institutions in the Black community be led and, wherever possible, staffed by Blacks. This is advisable psychologically, and it is necessary as a challenge to the myth that Black people are incapable of leadership. Admittedly, this violates the principle of egalitarianism ("We hire on the basis of merit alone, not color"). What Black and White America must understand is that egalitarianism is just a *principle* and it implies a notion of "color-blindness" which is deceptive. It must be clear by now that any society which has been color-conscious all its life to the detriment of a particular group cannot simply become color-blind and expect that group to compete on equal terms.

Black Power clearly recognizes the need to perpetuate color-consciousness, but in a positive way—to improve a group, not to subject it. When principles like egalitarianism have been so flagrantly violated for so long, it does not make sense to think that the victim of that violation can be equipped to benefit from opportunities simply upon their pronouncement. Obviously, some positive form of special treatment must be used to overcome centuries of negative special treatment.

This has been the argument of the Nation of Islam (the so-called Black Muslims) for years; it has also been the position of the National Urban League since its proposal for preferential treatment (the domestic Marshall Plan, which urged a "special effort to overcome serious disabilities resulting from historic handicaps") was issued at its 1963 Denver convention. This is not racism. It is not intended to penalize or subordinate another group; its goal is the positive uplift of a deliberately repressed group. Thus, when some Black Power advocates call for the appointment of Black people to head community action poverty programs and to serve as school principals, they have in mind the deliberate projection of

Blacks into positions of leadership. This is important to give other Black people a feeling of ability to achieve, if nothing else. And it is especially important for young Black children.

An example of concentrated special treatment is the plan some of us are proposing for a new approach to education in some of the Black ghettoes. It goes beyond the decentralization plans in the Bundy Report*; it goes beyond the community involvement at I.S. 201 in Harlem. It attempts to build on the idea proposed by Harlem CORE last year for an independent Board of Education for Harlem.

Harlem CORE and the New York Urban League saw the Bundy Report as a "step toward creating a structure which would bring meaningful education to the children of New York." CORE, led by Roy Innis, suggested an autonomous Harlem school system, chartered by the state legislature and responsible to the state. "It will be run by an elected school board and an appointed administrator, as most school boards are," CORE said. "The elected members will be Harlem residents. It is important that much of the detailed planning and structure be the work of the Harlem community." Funds would come from city, state, and federal governments and from private sources. In describing the long-range goal of the proposal CORE says: "Some have felt it is to create a permanently separate educational system. Others have felt it is a necessary step toward eventual integration. In any case, the ultimate outcome of this plan will be to make it possible for Harlem to choose."

Some of us propose that education in the Black community should be family oriented, not simply child oriented. In many of the vast urban Black Ghettoes (which will not be desegrated in the foreseeable future) the school should become the focal point of the community. This we call the Family-Community-School-Comprehensive Plan. School would cease to be a 9-to-3, September-to-June, time-off-for-good-behavior institution. It would involve education and training for the entire family—all year round, day and eve-

---

* After he left his position as President Lyndon Johnson's special assistant for security affairs in 1966, McGeorge Bundy became head of the Ford Foundation. The Foundation's report on the New York City school system appeared in November, 1967, and recommended its decentralization into about fifty autonomous community subsystems. The Intermediate School (I.S.) in New York is designed for grades 6–8.

ning. Black parents would be intimately involved as students, decision-makers, teachers. This is much more than a revised notion of adult education courses in the evening or the use of mothers as teachers' aides.

This plan would make the educational system the center of community life. We could have community health clinics and recreational programs built into the educational system. Above all, we could reorient the demeaning public welfare system, which sends caseworkers to "investigate" families. Why could we not funnel public assistance through the community educational program?

One major advantage would be the elimination of some of the bureaucratic chaos in which five to ten governmental agencies zero in on the Black family on welfare, seldom if ever coordinating their programs. The welfare department, for one, while it would not need to be altered in other parts of the state, would have to work jointly with the educational system in the Black community. This would obviously require administrative reorganization, which would not necessarily reduce bureaucracy but would consolidate and centralize it. In addition to being "investigators," for example, some caseworkers (with substantially reduced case loads) could become teachers of budgetary management, and family health consultants could report the economic needs of the family.

The teachers for such a system would be specially trained in a program similar to the National Teacher Corps, and recruits could include professionals as well as mothers who could teach classes in child-rearing, home economics, art music or any number of skills they obviously possess. Unemployed fathers could learn new skills or teach the ones they know. The curriculum would be both academic and vocational, and it would contain courses in the culture and history of Black people. The school would belong to the community. It would be a union of children, parents, teachers, social workers, psychologists, urban planners, doctors, community organizers. It would become a major vehicle for fashioning a sense of pride and group identity.

I see no reason why the local law-enforcement agency could not be integrated into this system. Perhaps this could take the form of training "community service officers," or junior policeman, as suggested in the report of the President's Commission on Civil Disorders. Or the local police precinct could be based in the school, working with the people on such things as crime prevention, first aid and the training of police officers. In this way, mutual trust could be developed between the Black community and the police.

Coordinating these programs could present problems to be worked out on the basis of the community involved, the agencies involved and the size of the system. It seems quite obvious that in innovation of this sort there will be a tremendous amount of chaos and uncertainty and there will be mistakes. This is understandable; it is the price to be paid for social change under circumstances of widespread alienation and deprivation. The recent furor about the Malcolm X memorial program at I.S. 201 in Harlem offers an example of the kind of problem to be anticipated. Rather than worrying about what one person said from a stage at a particular meeting, the authorities should be concerned about how the Board of Education will cooperate to transfer power to the community school board. When the transfer is made, confusion regarding lines of authority and program and curriculum content can be reduced.

The longer the delay in making the transfer, however, the greater the likelihood of disruption. One can expect misunderstanding, great differences of opinion and a relatively low return on efforts at the beginning of such programs. New standards of evaluation are being set, and the experimental concept developed at I.S. 201 should not be jeopardized by isolated incidents. It would be surprising if everything went smoothly from the outset.

Some programs *will* flounder, some will collapse out of sheer incompetence and faulty conception, but this presents an opportunity to build on mistakes. The precise details of the Comprehensive Plan would have to be worked out in conjunction with each community and agency involved. But the *idea* is seriously proposed. We must begin to think in entirely new terms of citizen involvement and decision-making.

Black Power has been accused of emphasizing decentralization, of overlooking the obvious trend toward consolidation. This is not true with the kind of Black Power described here, which is ultimately not separatist or isolationist. Some Black Power advocates are aware that this country is simultaneously experiencing centralization and decentralization. As the federal government becomes more involved (and it must) in the lives of people, it is imperative that we broaden the base of citizen participation. It will be the new forms, new agencies and structures developed by Black Power that will link these centralizing and decentralizing trends.

Black Power structures at the local level will activate people, instill faith (not alienation) and provide a habit of organization and consciousness of ability. Alienation will be overcome and trust in society restored. It will be through these local agencies that the centralized forces will operate, not through insensitive, unresponsive city halls. Billions of dollars will be needed each year, and these funds must be provided through a more direct route from their sources to the people.

Black Power is a developmental process; it cannot be an end in itself. To the extent that Black Americans can organize, and to the extent that White Americans can keep from panicking and begin to respond rationally to the demands of that organization— to that extent can we get on with the protracted business of creating not just law and order but a free and open society.

The Legacy of Slavery and the Roots of Black Nationalism*

Eugene D. Genovese

Eugene D. Genovese, professor of History at Sir George Williams University, has made notable contributions to the study of the history of the antebellum South. He is the author of *The Political Economy of Slavery*.

Slavery and its aftermath left the Blacks in a state of acute economic and cultural backwardness, with weak family ties and the much-discussed matriarchal preponderance. They also left a tradition of accommodation to paternalistic authority on the one hand, and a tradition of nihilistic violence on the other. Not docility or infantilization, but innocence of organized effort and political con-

---

* From Eugene D. Genovese, "The Legacy of Slavery and the Roots of Black Nationalism," *Studies on the Left* (November–December, 1966), 14–26. Reprinted by permission of the author.

sciousness plagued the Black masses and kept plaguing them well into the twentieth century. As a direct result of these effects and of the virtually unchallenged hegemony of the slaveholders, the Blacks had little opportunity to develop a sense of their own worth and had every opportunity to learn to despise themselves. The inability of the men during and after slavery to support their families adequately, and especially to protect their women from rape or abuse without forfeiting their own lives, has merely served as the logical end of an emasculating process.

The remarkable ascendancy of Booker T. Washington after the post-Reconstruction reaction must be understood against this backgrounds. We need especially to account for his enormous influence over the Black Nationalists who came after him. Washington tried to meet the legacy of slavery on its own terms. He knew that slavery had ill-prepared his people for political leadership; he therefore retreated from political demands. He knew that slavery had rendered manual labor degrading; he therefore preached the gospel of hard work. He knew that slavery has undermined the family and elementary moral standards; he therefore preached the whole gamut of middle-class virtues and manners. He knew his people had never stood on their own feet and faced the Whites as equals; he therefore preached self-reliance and self-help. Unhappily, apart from other ideological sins, he saw no way to establish self-reliance and self-respect except under the financial and social hegemony of the White upper classes. Somehow he meant to destroy the effects of paternalism in the long run by strengthening paternalism in the short run. It would be easy to say that he failed because of this tactic: but there is no way to be sure that the tactic was wrong in principle. He failed for other reasons, one of which was his reliance on the paternalistic, conservative classes at a time when they were rapidly losing power in the South to racist agrarian demagogues.

Washington's rivals did not, in this respect, do much better. The leaders of the NAACP repeatedly returned to a fundamental reliance on White leadership and money. Even Du Bois, in his classic critique of Washington, argued:

> While it is a great truth to say that the Negro must strive and strive mightily to help himself, it is equally true that unless his striving be not simply seconded, but rather aroused and en-

couraged by the initiative of the richer and wiser environing group, he cannot hope for great success.[1]

The differences between these militants and Washington's conservatives concerned emphases, tactics and public stance much more than ideological fundamentals. The differences were important, but their modest extent was no less so. The juxtaposition of the two tendencies reveals how little could be done even by the most militant without White encouragement and support. The wonder is that Black Americans survived the ghastly years between 1890 and 1920 at all. Survival—and more impressive, growing resistance to oppression—came at the price of continuing many phases of a paternalistic tradition that had already sapped the strength of the masses.

The conflict between Washington and Du Bois recalled many earlier battles between two tendencies that are still with us. The first has accepted segregation at least temporarily, has stressed the economic development of the Black community and has advocated self-help. This tendency generally prevailed during periods of retrogression in race relations until the upsurge of nationalism in our own day. Washington was its prophet; Black Nationalism has been its outcome. The second has demanded integration, has stressed political action and has demanded that Whites recognize their primary responsibility. Frederick Douglass was its prophet; the Civil Rights Movement has been its outcome. Yet, the lines have generally been blurred. Du Bois often sounded like a Nationalist and Washington probably would have thought Malcolm X a madman.[2] This blurring reflects the dilemma of the black community as a whole and of its bourgeoisie in particular: How do you integrate into a nation that does not want you? How do you separate from a nation that finds you too profitable to release?

To probe the relationship between this past and the recent upsurge of the Black masses requires more speculation and tentative judgment than one would like, but they cannot be avoided. Let us, at the risk of being schematic and one-sided, select features of

---

[1] W. E. B. Du Bois, *The Souls of Black Folk*, p. 53.

[2] For the period 1890–1915 see August Meier's careful and illuminating *Negro Thought in America: 1880–1915* (Ann Arbor: University of Michigan Press, 1963).

the developments of the last few decades and specially of the recent crisis for such analysis. In doing so let us bear in mind that the majority of Blacks today live outside the South; that they are primarily urban, not rural, in all parts of the country; that whole cities are on the way to becoming Black enclaves; that the problem increasingly centers on the urban North and West.[3] Let us bear in mind also that the only large-scale, organized Black mass movements until recently have been nationalist. Garvey commanded an organization of hundreds of thousands; the Muslims have tens of thousands and influence many more. No integrationist organization has ever acquired such numerical strength; none has ever struck such deep roots in the Black ghettoes.

Garvey's movement emphasized blackness as a thing of beauty, and struggled to convince the Black masses to repudiate White leadership and paternalism. The pompous titles, offices, uniforms and parades did and do evoke ridicule, but their importance lay, as Edmund David Cronon says, "in restoring the all but shattered Negro confidence." There was enormous ideological significance in Garvey's delightful description of a light-skinned mulatto opponent as "a White man passing for Negro."[4]

A decisive break with the White man's church, if not wholly with his religion, has formed a major part of Black Nationalist thinking. In view of the central role of anti-Christian ideology in the slave risings of Brazil and the Caribbean and the generally accommodationist character of American Christianity, this has been a rational response to a difficult problem. Garvey tried to

---

[3] For a perceptive discussion of these trends see Silberman, *Crisis in Black and White*, esp. pp. 7, 29–31.

[4] Edmund David Cronon, *Black Moses: The Story of Marcus Garvey and the Universal Negro Improvement Association* (Madison: University of Wisconsin Press, 1955, 1964), p. 174. It was never Garvey's intention to send all Blacks back to Africa; he wanted a strong African nation to serve as a protector to Blacks everywhere. See esp. the interview with Garvey in James Weinstein, ed., "Black Nationalism: The Early Debate," *Studies on the Left* (1964), 50–58.

The idea of Black nationality in America stretches back to the beginnings of the nineteenth century, if not earlier. See esp. Herbert Aptheker, "Consciousness of Negro Nationality to 1900," *Toward Negro Freedom* (New York: New Century Publishers, 1966), pp. 104–111; also Benjamin Quarles, *The Negro in the Making of America* (New York: 1964), p. 157.

organize his own African Orthodox Church. The Islam tendency, including Elijah Muhammed's Nation of Islam, has followed the maxim of Noble Drew Ali's Moorish Science Movement, "Before you can have a God, you must have a nationality." Garvey's Black Jesus and Muhammed's Allah have had many attributes of a tribal deity. Of special importance in Muhammed's teaching is his decidedly un-Islamic denial of an afterlife. In this way Black Muslim eschatology embodies a sharp reaction against accommodationist ideology. The tendency to turn away from the White man's religion has taken many forms, including conversion to Catholicism ostensibly because of its lack of a color line. In Catholic Brazil, on the other hand, an equivalent reason is given by Blacks who embrace Protestantism.[5]

Black Protestants in the United States have largely attended self-segregated churches since Reconstruction. With the collapse of Reconstruction these churches, especially in the South, played an increasingly accommodationist role, but they also served as community centers, protective agencies, marriage counseling committees and leadership training schools. As objective conditions changed, so did many ministers, especially the younger ones. One of the great ironies of the current struggle for integration has been the leading role played by ministers, whose training and following have been made possible by segregated organizations. The experience of the Protestant churches and their anti-Christian rivals brings us back to slavery's legacy of accommodationist but by no means necessarily treasonable leadership, of an absence of collective effort, of paternalistically induced dependence and of emasculation. Theoretically, a militant mass leadership could have arisen from sources other than enforced segregation; historically there seems to have been no other way.[6]

The first difficulty with the integrationist movement arises not from its ultimate commitment, which may or may not be desirable, but from the determined opposition of the Whites, whose hostility to close association with Blacks recedes slowly if at all. Integration may only mean desegration, and outstanding Black intellectuals

---

[5] Roger Bastide and Florestan Fernandes, *Brancos e negros em Sao Paulo* (2nd ed.; Sao Paulo: 1959), p. 254.

like Killens* and Baldwin insist that that is all they want it to mean; it need not mean assimilation. In fact, however, the line is difficult to hold, and segregationists probably do not err in regarding one as the prelude to the other. In any case, de facto segregation in education and housing is growing worse, and many of the professed goals of the Civil Rights Movement look further away than ever. Communities like Harlem face substantially the same social problems today as they did forty years ago.[7] I need not dwell on the worsening problem of Black unemployment and its implications.

Even where progress, however defined, occurs, the frustration of the Black masses deepens. The prosperity of recent decades has widened the gap between Blacks and Whites even of the same class. The rise of the African peoples has inspired Blacks here but has also threatened to open a gap in political power and dignity between Africans and Afro-Americans.[8]

---

[6] This recent experience, especially of SCLC, reveals the legacy of the past in other ways as well. Louis E. Lomax has criticized Dr. King for organizational laxness and has related the problems of the SCLC to the structure of the Baptist Church. "The Negro Baptist Church is a nonorganization. Not only is each congregation a sovereign body, dictated to by no one, but it would appear that the members who come together and form a Baptist Church are held together only by their mutual disdain for detailed organization and discipline." *The Negro Revolt* (New York: Signet, 1962), p. 86. As a result, according to Lomax, the SCLC is a loose, scattered organization that mobilizes itself only with great difficulty. Lomax makes good points but fails to note the extent to which this weakness flows from the entire history of Black America and especially the Black South. With justice, one could argue that the remarkable strength of SCLC in the face of this amorphousness is a singular tribute to Dr. King's political genius. He has mobilized masses who are ill-prepared for the kind of puritanical discipline preached by Elijah Muhammed.

* Oliver Killens, a contemporary novelist, headed the Harlem Writers' Workshop. His *Young Blood*, published in 1964, described the life of an average Negro in Georgia.

[7] Gilbert Osofsky, *Harlem: The Making of a Ghetto* (New York: Harper & Row, 1966), p. 179.

[8] See the perceptive remarks on these two kinds of gaps in Oscar Handlin, *Fire-Bell in the Night: The Crisis in Civil Rights* (Boston: Little, Brown and Co., 1964), pp. 21–22, 53; C. Eric Lincoln, *The Black Muslims in America* (Boston: Beacon, 1961), p. 45; and James Baldwin, *The Fire Next Time* (New York: Dell, 1964), pp. 105–106.

The resistance of Whites and the inflexibility of the social system constitute only half the problem. A. James Gregor, in an article published in *Science & Society* in 1963 analyzes an impressive body of sociological and psychological literature to demonstrate that integration under the disorderly conditions of American capitalist life more often than not undermines the development and dignity of the participating Blacks. He shows that the problems of the Black masses, in contradistinction to those of the bourgeoisie, become intensified by an integration which, in the nature of things, must pass them by. As Gregor demonstrates, Black Nationalism has been the political reply of these masses and especially of the working class.[9] Similarly, in his honest and thoughtful book, *Crisis in Black and White*, Charles E. Silberman analyzes cases such as that in New Rochelle, in which poor Black and rich White children had the wonderful experience of integrating in school. Why should anyone be surprised that the experiment proved a catastrophe for the Black children, who promptly lost whatever ambition they might have had.[10]

When liberals and academics speak of a "crisis of identity," they may sometimes merely wish to divert attention from the prior fact of oppression, but, by whatever name, that crisis exists. Slavery and its aftermath emasculated the Black masses; they are today profoundly sick and shaking with convulsions. It does us no good to observe, with Kardiner and Ovesey, that a psychology of oppression can only disappear when the oppression has disappeared.[11] It does us no good to admit that the sickness of White racism is more dangerous than the sickness it has engendered. We face an aroused, militant black community that has no intention of waiting for others to heal themselves. Those who believe that emasculation is the figment of the liberal imagination ought to read the words

---

[9] A. James Gregor, "Black Nationalism: A Preliminary Analysis of Negro Radicalism," *Science & Society* (Fall 1963), 415–432.

[10] Silberman, *Crisis in Black and White*, p. 298. Even under more favorable conditions, as John Oliver Killens has noted, Black children in the South often have a feeling of belonging that is undermined when they move north. *Black Man's Burden* (New York: Trident Press, 1965), pp. 84–85.

[11] Abram Kardiner and Lionel Ovesey, *The Mark of Oppression: Explorations in the Personality of the American Negro* (New York: Peter Smith, 1951, 1962), p. 387.

of any militant leader from David Walker to W. E. B. Du Bois, from Frederick Douglass to Martin Luther King, from Robert F. Williams to Malcolm X. The cry has been to assert manhood and renounce servility. Every outstanding black intellectual today— Killens, Baldwin, Ellison—makes the point in one way or another.* Let me quote only one, Ossie Davis on the death of Malcolm X:

> [Negroes knew] that Malcolm—whatever else he was or was not —*Malcolm was a man!*
>
> White folks do not need anybody to remind them that they are men. We do! This was his one incontrovertible benefit to his people. Protocol and common sense require that Negroes stand back and let the White man speak up for us, defend us, and lead us from behind the scene in our fight. This is the essence of Negro politics. But Malcolm said to hell with that! Get up off your knees and fight your own battles. That's the way to win back your self-respect. That's the way to make the White man respect you. And if he won't let you live like a man, he certainly can't keep you from dying like one.[12]

Is it any wonder, then, that Dr. King could write, almost as a matter of course, that the Blacks of Birmingham during the summer of 1963 shook off 300 years of psychological slavery and found their own worth?[13] It is no less instructive that his aide, the Reverend Wyatt T. Walker, denounced as "hoodlums" and "winos" those who responded to the attempt on King's life by attacking the White racists. King himself put it bluntly when he pleaded that the Black militant be allowed to march and sit-in, "If his repressed emotions do not come out in these nonviolent ways, they will come out in ominous expressions of violence."[14]

King and his followers apparently believe that concerted action for integration can cure the ills engendered by slavery and subsequent oppression and break down discrimination at the same time. In one sense they are right. Their greatest achievement has been to bring order and collective effort to a people who had learned little

---

* Ralph Ellison won the National Book Award in 1952 for his novel *Invisible Man.*

[12] Ossie Davis, "On Malcolm X," in *The Autobiography of Malcolm X* (New York: 1965), p. 435.

[13] Martin Luther King, Jr., *Why We Can't Wait*, p. 111.

[14] Silberman, *Crisis in Black and White*, pp. 122, 199.

of the necessity of either. But King must deliver victory or face grave consequences. As we have seen, not all slaves and freedman yielded meekly to the oppressor. Many fought, somtimes with great ferocity, but they generally fought by lashing out rather than by organized revolutionary effort. It would be the crowning irony if the civil Rights Movement has taught just enough of the lesson of collective effort to guarantee greater and more widespread nihilism in the wake of its inability to realize its program.

More and more young Black radicals are currently poring over Frantz Fanon's psychopathic panegyric to violence. Fanon argues that violence frees the oppressor from his inferiority complex and restores his self-respect.[15] Perhaps, but it is also the worst way to do either. Black Americans, like colonials, have always resorted to violence without accomplishing those goals. A slave who killed his overseer did not establish his manhood thereby—any wild animal can kill—he merely denied his docility. Violence can serve Fanon's purpose only when it is selective and disciplined—that is, political—but then it is precisely the collective effort, not the violence, that does the healing.[16]

The legend of Black docility threatens to betray those who perpetuate it. They are ill-prepared for the yielding of one side of the slave tradition—accommodation and servility—to the other side—antisocial nihilistic action. The failure of integration and the lawnessness to which the Blacks have for so long been subjected and subject combine to produce that result. James Baldwin and Malcolm X, especially in his remarks on the prestige of the ghetto

---

[15] Frantz Fanon, *The Wretched of the Earth* (New York: Grove Press, 1965). But see also two good critiques in *Studies on the Left* (May–June, 1966): Samuel Rohdie, "Liberation and Violence in Algeria," pp. 83–89, and esp. A. Norman Klein, "On Revolutionary Violence," pp. 62–82.

[16] The warning of so humane and sensitive a man as Killens on this matter is worth quoting: "The advocates of absolute non-violence have reckoned without the psychological needs of Black America. Let me state it plainly: There is in many Negroes a deep need to practice violence against their White tormentors." *Black Man's Burden*, p. 113. The Muslims understand this very well, as does Dr. King; they try to substitute internal discipline and collective effort for the violence itself.

hustler, have each warned of this danger.[17] Bayard Rustin has made a similar point with gentle irony:

> From the point of view of motivation, some of the healthiest Negro youngsters I know are juvenile delinquents vigorously pursuing the American Dream of material acquisition and status, yet finding the conventional means of attaining it blocked off, they do not yield to defeatism but resort to illegal (and sometimes ingenious) methods. They are not alien to American culture.[18]

Those historians who so uncritically admire the stealing of hogs and smashing of plows by slaves might consider its modern equivalent. In the words of Silberman:

> There are other means of protest, of course: misbehaving in school, or dropping out of school altogether; not showing up for work on time, or not showing up at all (and lying about the reason); breaking school windows or ripping telephone receivers out of outdoor booths; or the oldest form of protest of all, apathy —a flat refusal to cooperate with the oppressor or to accept his moral code.[19]

Black nationalism, in its various manifestations, constitutes a necessary response on the part of the Black masses. The Muslims for example, have understood the inner needs of the working-class Blacks who have filled their ranks and have understood the futility —for these people at least—of integrationist hopes. Their insistence on the forcible assertion of a dignified, disciplined, collectively responsible Black community represents a rational response to a harsh reality.[20] We need not dwell on what is unrealistic, romantic

---

[17] Baldwin, *The Fire Next Time*, pp. 35–37; *The Autobiography of Malcolm X*, pp. 315–316.

[18] Rustin, Bayard, "From Protest to Politics: The Future of the Civil Rights Movement," in Frances L. Broderick and August Meier, eds., *Negro Protest Thought in the Twentieth Century*, p. 410.

[19] Silberman, *Crisis in Black and White*, pp. 47–48.

[20] The best study of the Muslims is E. U. Essien-Udom, *Black Nationalism: A Search for Identity in America* (New York: Dell, 1964). Elijah Muhammed has demonstrated remarkable awareness of the persistence of the slave tradition, even in its most elusive forms. His denunciation of Black conspicuous consumption, for example, correctly views it as essentially a reflection of the mores of the slaveholders and counterposes to it standards that recall those of revolutionary petty-bourgeois puritanism.

or even reactionary in the Nation of Islam or other nationalist groups; they are easy to see. Ralph Bunche, in his radical days, Gunnar Myrdal and many others have for years pointed out that the idea of a separate Black economy is a will-o-the-wisp and that the idea of a separate territory is less than that. Yet I am not sure how to answer Marc Schleifer who in 1963 asked whether these goals were less realistic than those of equality under capitalism or a socialist revolution in the foreseeable future.[21] I am not sure, either, that Malcolm X, Harold W. Cruse and Stokely Carmichael have not been wiser than their Marxist critics in demanding Black ownership of everything in Harlem.[22] Such ownership will do little toward the creation of a Black economy, but many of its advocates are easily bright enough to know as much. The point is that it may, as Malcolm X suggested, play a decisive role in the establishment of community stability and self-respect.

The Black struggle for equality in America has always had two tendencies—integrationist and separatist—and it is likely to retain both. Since a separate economy and national territory are not serious possibilities, the struggle for economic integration will undoubtedly be pressed forward. For this reason alone some degree of unity between the civil-rights and nationalist tendencies may be expected. The Black bourgeoisie and its allied stratum of skilled and government clerical workers will certainly continue its fight for integration, but the interest of the Black workers in this fight, is, at bottom, even greater. At the same time there will clearly be serious defeats, as well as some victories, and the slogan "Freedom Now!" may soon turn to ashes.

The cumulative problems of past and present nonetheless demand urgent action. The assertion of Black hegemony in specific cities and districts—Nationalism if you will—offers the only politically realistic hope of transcending the slave heritage. First, it seems the only way for Black communities to police themselves, to curb antisocial elements and to enforce adequate health and

---

[21] Marc Schleifer, "Socialism and the Negro Movement," *Monthly Review* (September, 1963), 225–228.

[22] For a suggestive theoretical defense of such a demand see Harold W. Cruse, "Revolutionary Nationalism and the Afro-American," *Studies on the Left*, II, no. 3 (1962), 12–25; and his subsequent communication in III, no. 1 (1962), esp. p. 70. See also *The Autobiography of Malcolm X*, p. 318.

housing standards, and yet break with paternalism and instill pride and a sense of worth. Second, it seems the best way to build a position of strength from which to fight for a proper share of jobs and federal funds as a matter of right not privilege. Black Nationalism may yet prove to be the only force capable of restraining the impulse to violence, of disciplining Black rebelliousness and of absorbing the nihilistic tradition into a socially constructive movement. If this seems like a conservative rendering of an ostensibly revolutionary movement, I can only answer that there are no ingredients for a successful, independent Black revolution, and that Black Nationalism can ultimately go only a few steps further to the left than the White masses. The rise of specifically Black cities, counties and districts, with high-quality Black schools, well-paid teachers, as well as political leaders, churches and community centers, could and should uproot the slave tradition once and for all, could and should act as a powerful lever for structural reform of the American economy and society.

I do not offer these remarks as a program for a Black movement, for the time is past when White men can offer programs to Black militants. They are, happily, no longer listening. But I do submit that they are relevant to the formation of a program for ourselves—for the American left. If this analysis has merit, the demands of the Black community will increasingly swing away from the traditional appeal to federal power and toward the assertion of local and regional autonomy. Even now Bayard Rustin and others warn that federal troops can only preserve the status quo. I should observe, further, that the appeals to Washington reflect the convergence of two powerful and debilitating traditions: slave-engendered paternalistic dependence and the growing state paternalism of White America. Let us admit that the naive fascination of leftists for centralized power has, since the 1930's, greatly strengthened this tendency. With such labels as "progressive" and even "socialist," corporate liberalism has been building what William Appleman Williams has aptly called a nonterroristic totalitarian society. Yet American socialism has never even posed a theoretical alternative. When Professor Williams called for a program and local reassertion and opposition to centralization, he was dismissed by most radicals as a Utopian of doubtful mental competence. We may now rephrase his question: How do we propose to support an increasingly nationalistic Black radicalism, with its demands for local hegemony, unless we have an ideology and program of opposition to the centralization of state power?

The possible courses for the Black Liberation Movement include a total defeat in an orgy of violence (we ought to remember that there is nothing inevitable in its or our victory), a compromise with imperialism in return for some degree of local rule or the integration of its bourgeois strata, and the establishment of Black Power on the basis of a developing opposition to America capitalism. Since its future depends to a great extent on the progress of its integrationist struggle for a place in the economy, the Black community must for a while remain well to the left of the current liberal consensus by its demands for public works and structural reform. But reform could occur under the auspices of an expansion rather than a contraction of state centralization, and the most militant of the Black leaders may have to settle for jobs and local political control in return for allegiance to a consolidating national and international empire. The final result will be decided by the struggle within White America, with the Blacks playing the role of an increasingly independent ally for one or another tendency. Notwithstanding some ofiensive and pretentious rhetoric, the advocates of Black Power have judged their position correctly. They are determined to win control of the ghettoes, and we would be foolish not to bet on them. The use to which they put that power, however, depends not on our good wishes or on their good intentions, but on what they are offered as a *quid pro quo*. For American socialism the Black revolt opens an opportunity for relevance that has been missing for decades. What we do with that opportunity, as the leaders of SNCC have rather rudely reminded us, is our problem, not theirs.